Asset/
Liability
Management
Techniques

by
Bill Williams

with
Charlene G. Valenza
Principal Research Manager
Bank Administration Institute

Bank Administration Institute

Rolling Meadows, Illinois

Bank Administration Institute

BAI is a unique professional services organization that offers research, information services, and professional development opportunities to bankers worldwide.

The Institute's independent, not-for-profit status enables it to serve bankers objectively—as both adviser and analyst. Through the Foundation for Financial Institutions Research, an Institute affiliate, BAI has strengthened its ability to analyze policies and issues that are more strategic in scope and effect.

BAI is a creative partnership, blending the policy-level experience of bankers worldwide with the specialized expertise of its professional staff. These bankers serve on the Institute's board of directors, technical commissions and advisory groups, ensuring that BAI meets changing needs with relevant programs and services.

The Institute presents information across a wide range of critically important areas, including management and administration; strategic planning; accounting, finance and control; audit and tax; corporate financial services; retail financial services; marketing; and operations and technology. This information is conveyed through methods well-suited to the varying needs of banking professionals—ranging from research, technical conferences, and educational programs to a broad and growing array of publications.

Library of Congress Catalog Card Number: 88-70051
Copyright © 1988 by Bank Administration Institute, Rolling Meadows, Illinois. All rights reserved. This book or any parts of it may not be reproduced in any form without written permission from the publisher.
Printed in the United States of America
No. 363   ISBN: 1-55520-033-8

Contents

List of Figures	vii
List of Tables	ix
Introduction	1
1 Matching Techniques	**7**
Matching Defined	7
Gap Measurement and Projection Techniques	9
Gap Measurement Concepts	10
Gap Profiles	12
The Simulation Technique	16
The Duration Analysis Technique	17
Immediate Matching Actions	18
Long-Range Matched Funding	21
Liquidity Considerations	22
Summary	23
2 Swap Techniques	**27**
Types of Swap Structures	28
Interest Rate Swaps	29
The Costs Involved	31
Advantages of Swaps	32
Factors in the Swap Decision	35
Swap Implementation	39
Credit Considerations in Swap Transactions	42
Measuring Interest Rate Risk Exposure in Swaps	45
The Projection Approach	46
The Formula Approach	47
Accounting for Swaps	48
Variations on the Theme	50
Summary	51

CONTENTS

3	**Futures as a Hedging Technique**	53
	Forwards	54
	Futures as Types of Forwards	55
	How Futures Work	57
	Interest Rates on Futures Contracts	60
	Characteristics of Futures Contracts	61
	Standardized Contracts	61
	Liquidity	62
	Flexibility and Ease of Use	63
	Low Cost	64
	Futures Versus Swaps	64
	Basis and Basis Risk	66
	Designing the Hedge Decision-Making Process	69
	Defining the Risk	71
	Selecting the Appropriate Futures Contract	72
	Selecting the Contract Month	74
	Determining the Hedge Ratio	76
	Sample Hedge Ratio Application	78
	Conversion Factor Hedge Technique	83
	The Duration Hedge Technique	88
	Calculating Duration	88
	Summary	91
4	**Options as Hedges**	95
	Roles of the Parties to an Option	96
	Exchange-Traded and Custom Options	99
	Determining Option Status	100
	Elements of the Option Premium	102
	Using Options as Hedges	103
	Accounting for Options	107
	Summary	107

5	**Effective Portfolio Management**	111
	Why the Portfolio Is Important	112
	Portfolio Objectives	114
	The Necessary Training	118
	Liquidity and the Portfolio	119
	Additional Portfolio Management Concepts	123
	The Portfolio and the Tax Position	126
	Summary	127
Conclusion		131
Index		137

List of Figures

1	Graphic Representation of Various Gap Profiles	15
2	Interest Rate Swap	30
3	The Variable Rate Received	34
4	Comparison of Prime, Six-Month LIBOR, and 90-Day T-Bill Rates	38
5	Elements of a Futures Contract	58
6	Financial Futures—Basis	67
7	Sample Hedge Ratio Problem Schematic	80
8	Using the Hedge Ratio Technique	82
9	Conversion Factor Hedges	84
10	Comparision of Cash and Futures Market Hedges	87
11	Duration—Hedging the Gap	90
12	Elements of an Option	96

List of Tables

1	Sample Gap Profile Worksheet	14
2	Typical Net Cost of a Swap	37
3	Market Interest Increases Result in Corresponding Increases in LIBOR	37
4	Interest Rate Risk Exposure	48

Introduction

Asset and liability (A/L) management has become increasingly critical in every bank's profit strategy. Its objectives are to:

- Manage the portfolio in a manner consistent with the bank's investment policy.
- Obtain the desired earnings while holding risk at acceptable levels.
- Maintain adequate liquidity at a cost consistent with earnings goals.

Both on- and off-balance sheet investments must be considered in A/L management, since all investments contribute to the success or failure of this effort.

The bank's policy toward risk-taking is a key determinant of the tools available to the A/L and/or portfolio manager. This policy often dictates when to take action to minimize potential losses and what specific actions to take. While some risk is present in virtually any investment, the amount and nature of risk taken depends on what is acceptable to bank management.

Interest and Earnings Projections

Interest-rate risk and its effects on earnings must be an integral factor in determining the acceptable risk level. Market interest rate projections must be available on a regular basis for optimum A/L management. The effects of rate fluctuations depend on the bank's position at the time — whether it is asset- or liability-sensitive. When the bank is in an asset-sensitive (positive) position, it has assets repricing faster than liabilities, and its earnings usually increase with rising interest rates. Conversely, market interest rate increases result in reduced earnings when the bank is liability-sensitive. To the extent that it can project future interest rates successfully and adjust its asset and liability holdings accordingly, the bank can control its earnings position.

The difference between rate-sensitive assets and rate-sensitive liabilities is called *gap*, or *mismatch*. Gap can be projected on the level of bank activities and can be controlled, or adjusted up or down, by adding investments (assets or liabilities) to the portfolio. Several techniques are available for making gap projections, including:

- Profiles that indicate the bank's potential earnings positions in different time frames if specific changes are made in the composition of the portfolio.
- Computer-based models that help the bank make earnings projections in a large number of asset and liability positions.
- Duration analysis techniques that take into consideration the effects of principal reductions (cash flows) on long-term assets and liabilities.

To be meaningful, each of these techniques and its results must be related to projected market interest rates at various future times. Ideally, decisions are made by an *Asset and Liability Committee (ALCO)* whose role includes keeping the bank abreast of trends, projections, and investment portfolio management techniques. Based on timely, accurate projections of interest rate movements and their effects on earnings, the ALCO and bank management can determine what steps to take to attain satisfactory earnings within acceptable risk limits. Measurement techniques and their ap-

INTRODUCTION

plications are discussed fully in two other Bank Administration Institute books: *Asset/Liability Measurement Techniques* and *The How-To of Duration Analysis*.[1] Therefore, measurement techniques are discussed only briefly here. This book concentrates on the steps that can be taken to manage the portfolio effectively based on the projections obtained from whatever measurement tools the bank uses.

Potential A/L Management Tools

The portfolio manager has several tools available for use in portfolio (investment) management. They include:

- *Matching assets and liabilities*. This is an effort to maintain the *status quo* of the overall investment position. If management is satisfied with the earnings picture as it stands and wants to maintain it into the future, matching techniques (in which assets are funded by similar offsetting liabilities) help accomplish this long-term objective.

- *Swaps*. This technique involves exchanging interest payments to assure adequate funding or to gain a more advantageous interest rate position. When swaps are made, caution must be exercised to avoid putting the bank in an adverse tax position. In general, however, swaps are often an effective way to protect against unfavorable interest rate swings while enabling a bank to maintain adequate liquidity.

- *Futures*. These instruments provide a means of reducing the risk involved in a current or planned market transaction by enabling the manager to make an off

---

[1] Bill Williams. *Asset/Liability Measurement Techniques*. Rolling Meadows, Illinois: Bank Administration Institute, 1987 and *The How-To of Duration Analysis*. Rolling Meadows, Illinois: Bank Administration Institute.

setting transaction in the futures market. True speculators in the futures market do not have the advantage of the offsetting current or planned cash market transaction. Therefore, the speculator's risk is much greater, but so is the possibility of earning a higher yield on the investment. It is unlikely that bank portfolio managers would be involved in futures speculation. Rather, they would use futures as hedges to offset risks presented by current or planned spot market transactions.

- *Options*. The buyer of an option contract obtains the right to buy or sell one or more underlying financial instruments (or other items, e.g., an amount of foreign currency) at a specified price during a stated time. For this right, the buyer pays a premium (fee) to the seller. By fixing the price of the underlying financial instruments, the buyer can hedge against interest rate risk exposure presented by other items in the portfolio.

The exact mix of A/L management tools used depends on the bank's short- and long-term goals and objectives.

Selecting the Proper Tools

Investment philosophy often has a direct bearing on the degree of confidence that a bank's depositors and stockholders have. The A/L and portfolio manager(s) must be fully aware of the organization's preferred approach to its investments. This knowledge is essential if the portfolio is to be managed successfully while remaining within senior management's guidelines. For this and other reasons (including attracting investors and demonstrating a sincere effort to conform to all banking regulations), the bank's management team is probably wise to establish a formal, clearly worded investment policy.

INTRODUCTION

Bank stockholders expect and deserve a return on their investment. The bank's investment policy must not be so restrictive as to hamper the portfolio manager's efforts to achieve a reasonable earnings level. Balance must be attained between the degree of risk the bank is willing to take and the desired or anticipated profit level. A/L management, much of which, in this regard, is portfolio management, is the ongoing effort to reach and maintain that balance.

With a stated investment policy as a guideline, the portfolio manager can select and use the appropriate management tools. Some of the tools discussed here are used most effectively to attain short-term goals, while others are better suited for meeting long-range objectives that extend two or more years into the future. While nearly all investments entail some risk, the portfolio manager, with the guidance of the ALCO and senior management, can limit risk to levels that remain within the confines of the bank's stated policy.

Summary

Senior management must establish specific policies concerning investments and earnings. Analysis of where the bank stands today coupled with realistic, attainable earnings goals enables the bank to plan well into the future.

These determinations can only be made successfully when the A/L management team is able to provide senior management with accurate, timely projections of interest-rate risks, liquidity sources and uses, and the effects of these variables on overall earnings. These projections help management decide where it wants to be at various times in the future.

It then becomes the responsibility of the A/L management team, including the investment and portfolio managers, to see that the bank attains those goals. Steps are taken either to maintain the *status quo* or to change the bank's position, depending on what best fits the policy the organization has established.

How well this effort succeeds depends, in part, on the portfolio managers' abilities to select and use the appropriate investment/portfolio management tools and techniques. This book explains the tools and techniques and how to use them.

1
Matching Techniques

Most banks' investment policies tend to support a sound, conservative position that promotes stability by minimizing risk. The use of matching techniques in portfolio management is one means by which stability is maintained.

Matching Defined

Matching is an effort to keep the maturity, interest rate, and liquidity characteristics of the assets and liabilities in the portfolio roughly matched at all times. This is accomplished by match-funding each asset with a liability of equal maturity, preferably at a favorable spread. The objective is not necessarily to minimize the gap (the difference between rate-sensitive assets and rate-sensitive liabilities), but to maintain it approximately at a constant level. If market interest rates move in the directions and amounts anticipated by the bank, then the organization can predict its position in terms of earnings on its investment portfolio. It probably will not experience extreme gains in interest earnings, but neither will it suffer significant losses due to unexpected movements in interest rates. Matching is a "middle-of-the-road" investment philosophy, and it can effectively keep the bank's portfolio in balance irrespective of changes in interest rates.

To implement and maintain a successful matching policy, a bank constantly must be alert to several critical factors, including:

- *The bank's current asset and liability position.* If there are more rate-sensitive assets than liabilities in the portfolio, then the bank is in a positive mismatch (gap) position. Conversely, if the portfolio contains more rate-sensitive liabilities than assets, the position is considered negative.

Neither situation is necessarily bad or good from an earnings standpoint, since the prevailing interest rate in relation to the bank's position is actually the deciding factor.

- *The bank's projected asset and liability position.* If current trends continue, will that position remain the same? Is it better to change the bank's position by increasing or decreasing the asset or liability holdings in the portfolio? If the bank wants to maintain as closely matched a portfolio as possible, the gap remains essentially the same, even though the volumes in both categories can increase or decrease dramatically.

- *Current and projected interest rates.* The bank must make certain that current portfolio performance, which is directly affected by market interest rates, reflects the desired management philosophy. If it does not, what steps can be taken to improve that performance based on projected interest movements? The ALCO must provide senior management with its best estimates of where interest rates are likely to be at the end of this month, next month, and a year or more from now. This will enable the management team to determine, with the ALCO's guidance, what position to attempt to be in at each projected time.

These are the critical factors in maintaining any gap position, whether or not a matching effort is being made. The effects of prevailing interest rates at various times depend on the bank's asset/liability position in each time frame. Timely, accurate gap and interest rate projections are required for establishing or maintaining specific investment positions—here, a matched portfolio.

Gap Measurement and Projection Techniques

There are three commonly used gap measurement or projection techniques:

- *The gap profile approach*, in which assets and liabilities are assigned to time buckets based on their maturities. Gap is the difference between the rate-sensitive assets and the rate-sensitive liabilities in the portfolio, based on their repricing characteristics. With a matching philosophy of portfolio management, the objective is to maintain the gap at approximately the same level, even though the volumes and maturities of the specific assets and liabilities in the portfolio change.
- *Simulation models* that enable the ALCO to project a wide range of possible interest rate and A/L position scenarios. This projection technique is best applied with the use of computers. It simplifies the ALCO's task of making management aware of asset and liability positions that might be experienced and what effect various interest rates would have on each position, given different scenarios.
- *Duration analysis*, a method that takes cash flows on assets and liabilities into consideration in projecting potential positions. This technique works best for long-term assets and liabilities, such as mortgage loans.

Note that liquidity is not mentioned in the above discussion. Gap measurement techniques can influence a bank's projected liquidity position, but do not measure it. Liquidity is important to every bank, regardless of investment philosophy; and it must be tracked in terms of both sources and uses. A bank that is interested in maintaining asset and liability *status quo* through matching techniques will be most interested in keeping approximately the same liquidity position. Steps that might be taken to accomplish this are discussed later in this section.

Gap Measurement Concepts

As noted, gap is the difference between rate-sensitive assets (RSA) and rate-sensitive liabilities (RSL) in a bank's portfolio. In formula form:

$$\text{Gap} = \text{RSA} - \text{RSL}$$

$$\text{Gap Ratio} = \frac{\text{RSA}}{\text{RSL}}$$

A bank's position is stated as asset-sensitive (greater amount of rate-sensitive assets) or liability-sensitive (greater amount of rate-sensitive liabilities) depending on the types and volumes of investments its portfolio contains. When the portfolio is asset-sensitive, the bank is said to be in a positive gap position; when the portfolio is liability-sensitive, the bank is in a negative gap position.

Either position can have a favorable or an adverse effect on earnings because: *When a positive gap exists, earnings move in the same direction as interest rates; with a negative position, earnings movement is opposite to rate movement.* A positive gap at a given point in time is not always beneficial to earnings, as its name might lead one to think. A positive position results in *decreased* earnings when rates fall. This is because, as noted, earnings follow rate movement when a positive gap exists.

If a bank is heavily asset-sensitive (in a strong positive position) because of a preponderance of large commercial and other loans, for example, a decrease in rates means that the bank will charge a lower rate on these loans to remain competitive. While some loans may be locked in to a fixed rate that protects the bank's interest income on those assets, most large commercial loans today are tied to prime and are, therefore, variable-rate by definition. As a general statement, earnings decrease if the bank is in a positive position and interest rates fall.

That same position provides increased earnings, however, if interest rates rise. The same fixed-rate loans that helped protect at least some of the bank's earnings in a falling interest rate situation now serve as a detriment, since the cost of money (the prevailing interest rate) may actually exceed the rates applicable to the fixed-rate loans in the portfolio. Since variable-rate loans are more prevalent today, however, earnings of a bank in a positive position generally rise with increasing interest rates.

Just the opposite statements are true when the bank is in a negative gap position. When prevailing interest rates rise, the bank must pay more for money it is using, and earnings decrease. And if rates should fall while the bank is in a negative position, earnings increase because the bank is paying less for (or on) those liabilities than it was prior to the rate change.

Clearly, the bank wishing to maintain a matched portfolio of offsetting assets and liabilities (or any other stated position, for that matter) must be especially concerned with its position when interest rates move up or down. Armed with accurate interest rate movement projections, the bank can set out to position itself to take advantage of prevailing rates in various future time frames. With a stated middle-of-the-road philosophy, however, the bank probably would not make unilateral changes in either side (asset or liability) of its portfolio holdings. Rather, it would attempt to hold a more static gap position, thereby keeping earnings at about the same relative level.

ASSET/LIABILITY MANAGEMENT TECHNIQUES

This approach keeps portfolio managers busy, since they must add liabilities to offset acquired assets, and vice-versa. Maintaining a generally matched position may be no easy task when the objective is to acquire or liquidate assets that roughly equal added or deleted liabilities. Special problems can occur when certain general activities lead to a rapid increase or decrease in a given area. For example, when CD rates move up quickly, depositors may remove unusually large amounts from their savings accounts to take advantage of the higher earnings. This sudden depletion of a major liability may take some time to offset. If interest rates are particularly erratic at the time, the bank's earnings may be affected, at least temporarily.

Possibilities such as this emphasize the importance of timely, accurate interest rate projections. The three measurement techniques discussed here, coupled with accurate interest rate projections, can provide a solid framework for asset/liability management.

Gap Profiles

The gap profile measurement tool involves placing the bank's assets and liabilities into "buckets," based on their maturities. For greatest effectiveness, profiles should extend at least a year into the future. Two, three, or more years often prove even more helpful. Those items with "overnight" and up to 30-day maturities are placed in the nearest bucket; those that mature, or reprice, within 60 days in the next bucket, and so on.

The objective of a gap profile is to provide a picture of the amounts of assets and liabilities that will be maturing during defined time frames. The recommended maturity (repricing) buckets are established for relatively short (often 30- or 60-day) periods extending out to a year, then at least annually after that. Decisions can then be made as to whether to replace these items with similar securities, use the money (or replace it) in a particular manner, or go a different direction altogether. The knowledge provided by the profiles enables the bank to plan its investment (portfolio) strategy in line with its stated management objectives.

The information concerning the asset/liability gap, or mismatch, in each time frame (bucket) must then be viewed from the standpoint of projected interest rates at those points. For example, if a bank is currently in a positive gap position, but will have several large assets maturing in the 90-day time bucket, it must decide, based on the projected interest rate in that period, whether it wants to maintain this positive position. If its stated policy is to maintain a matched position, any replacement of those assets must be considered in terms of the offsetting liabilities. Therefore, the liabilities that are scheduled to reprice in that same bucket must also be considered.

To project its gap using the profile technique, a bank must first establish the buckets and place its assets and liabilities into them according to their repricing dates. This can be accomplished using a worksheet similar to the one shown in Table 1. In this illustration, the bank anticipates that it will move from a positive to a negative position as various volumes of assets and liabilities mature. Based on this projected gap profile, it knows it must replace a certain amount of assets in each of the indicated time frames if it is to match the liabilities in the portfolio and maintain the desired gap position.

With a policy other than matched funding, the bank might decide to allow the anticipated negative position to occur, especially if it also anticipates a decrease in market interest

Table 1
Sample Gap Profile Worksheet

	0-30 Days	30-90 Days	90-180 Days	180-360 Days	Over 360 Days
Assets					
Commercial loans	150	25	10	15	50
Consumer loans	5	10	15	20	75
Securities	25	25			50
Nonearning					25
TOTAL	180	60	25	35	200
Liabilities					
Core deposits	25	50	75		100
CDs	50	50	50		
Borrowings	50				
Noninterest bearing					50
TOTAL	125	100	125	0	150
Net mismatch	55	(40)	(100)	35	
Cumulative—$	55	15	(85)	(50)	
—% of Assets	11%	3%	(17%)	(10%)	

rates during those time frames. The negative (liability-sensitive) position in which the bank expects to find itself in the 30-90 days and 90-180 days buckets would provide increased earnings if interest rates did, in fact, decrease. Since the objective of a matching policy is to maintain the *status quo* of the gap, however, the obvious move is to acquire additional assets to replace those that are repricing in those time frames. This move is most appropriate when no decrease (or perhaps even an increase) is anticipated in market interest rates.

Cumulative gap profiles also can be presented in graphic form, as illustrated in Figure 1. In Profile A, the bank anticipates that the gap will remain steady. This will be the case if a matching policy is adhered to and the portfolio is managed accordingly. Profile B illustrates a situation in which a negative (liability-sensitive) gap is anticipated within the next 90 days, after which it remains relatively steady. In Profile C, it is anticipated that the gap will become increasingly negative out to the six-month time bracket, then will become less negative thereafter. The fourth profile (D) indicates an anticipated shift from a positive to a negative gap position, with some variation (but still negative) through the entire projected time frame. With Profiles B, C, and

Figure 1
Graphic Representation of Various Gap Profiles

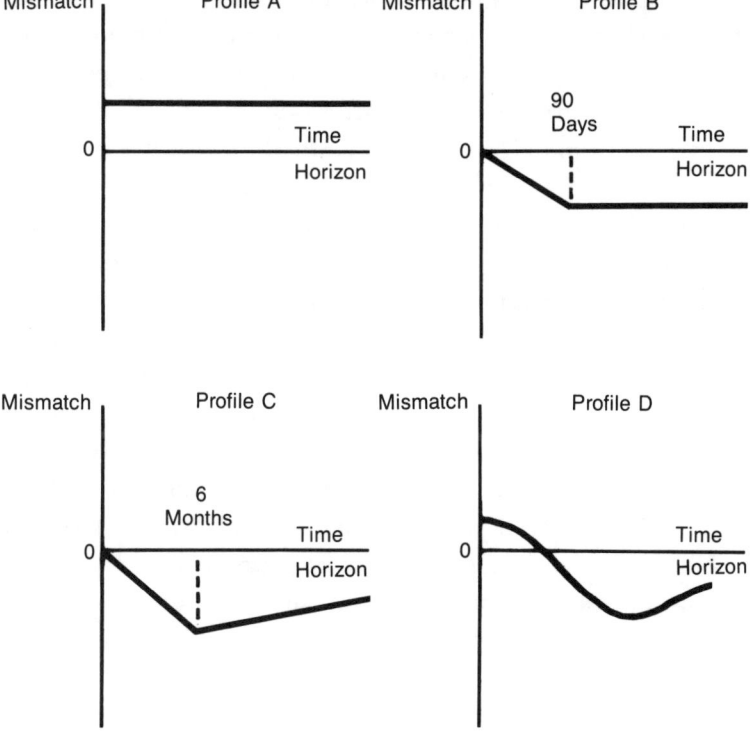

ASSET/LIABILITY MANAGEMENT TECHNIQUES

D, the bank will have to take action, adding assets to and/or deleting liabilities from its portfolio, if it wants to maintain a positive gap position through a matched-funding approach.

The Simulation Technique

The simulation technique of gap measurement involves preparation of a range of possible scenarios that present various asset and liability positions and market interest rate projections over several time frames. If the bank uses a computer to perform this task, an extremely wide range of potential scenarios can be developed and presented in both verbal and graphic forms. The software and computer requirements may or may not be practical in a given bank's situation. Even without the aid of a computer, however, several potential gap and interest rate scenarios can be developed and presented to management as an added tool for use in directing the organization's investment activities.

The range of "what ifs" that can be calculated into various simulation models can be tremendous. So some limitations are necessary from a practical standpoint. One approach is to project the worst, best, and most likely cases for management review. A number of possible variations can be built into the system, but management will probably be most interested in projections that portray likely situations. The ALCO, with the help of the portfolio manager and other personnel involved in investment activities, must decide which of the many potential situations are most likely to exist at various future points. These possibilities can then be used as a guideline in deciding how to manage the bank's portfolio.

The Duration Analysis Technique

Both profile and simulation modeling measurement techniques fail to take into consideration periodic payments that are received on assets and amounts that must be paid to satisfy liabilities in the portfolio. In other words, these gap projection methods ignore the cash flows that occur with both assets and liabilities. This can provide false risk assessments, especially on assets and liabilities whose maturities (repricing dates) extend several years into the future.

In an ideal matching situation, a given asset is matched (funded) with a liability that has the same maturity. The bank tries to effect this match at a favorable spread, positive or negative, depending on anticipated interest rate fluctuations. But the final maturity dates and values of these instruments are really insufficient factors in obtaining a true match-funded stance, because they do not take into consideration the periodic cash flows generated by the asset side of the match.

One definition of duration is the average time required to recover cost on an investment. Since an asset generates cash flows at specified times over its lifetime, a true picture of duration (time needed to recover cost) is only presented when these amounts are measured. Higher-yield instruments produce higher periodic cash flows, and these serve to shorten the duration of these investments. In short, costs are recovered more rapidly with higher-yield assets on which greater periodic cash flows are received.

Duration analysis should be considered for use as an A/L measurement tool whenever the bank's portfolio contains large blocks of long-term assets and liabilities (e.g., mortgage loans, very long-term CDs, and bonds with extended maturities) on which there are periodic cash flows. This technique will work even in the absence of a preponderance of long-term assets and liabilities. However, in this case, the entire portfolio is considered, not just individual instruments.

Immediate Matching Actions

A combination of gap measurement techniques, used with a range of potential market interest rate projections, can provide most banks with a reasonably accurate estimate of their future earnings positions under various conditions. While no one can say with total accuracy exactly what prevailing interest rates will be at any future point, experience and the nature of the business/economic environment today—considered along with trends that may or may not continue into the future—can certainly provide a reasonable estimate. A bank can then use these projections as the basis for investment actions that will assure its matching philosophy is adhered to and that its earnings are adequately protected.

If a bank owns a large block of government bonds that are set to mature some 180 days from now, it has probably matched this asset with an offsetting block of liabilities with approximately the same maturity—CDs, for example. With these matched assets and liabilities maturing (repricing) in the same bucket, the bank's asset/liability gap will remain essentially unchanged, assuming no other major factors affect the balance. As a percentage, earnings also will be unaffected. In actual dollar amounts, however, earnings can be affected tremendously—perhaps adversely—unless another set of matched assets and liabilities, adding up to approximately the same total volumes, is brought into the portfolio in the same time frame. The projection techniques used by the bank indicate where (in what time frames) action will be necessary to maintain a matched position without adversely affecting total earnings.

MATCHING TECHNIQUES

Not all investment activities can be quite so planned, however. There may be occasions when a bank can take advantage of a fast-breaking investment opportunity to make a reasonably safe, but relatively high return. Or a previously unannounced bond issue that fits into a bank's investment planning suddenly becomes available. Even though the objective is to maintain a matched position, investment personnel cannot afford to pass up attractive opportunities. Therefore, the decision is made—often by the portfolio manager with fast approval from one or two other officers—to make the investment.

Temporarily, at least, the balance between assets and liabilities has been upset. The portfolio manager has added a sizable asset (or liability, since they, too, occasionally offer opportunities to attain specific investment goals) to the portfolio. Now, however, the matched-funding directive indicates that an offsetting liability must be brought into the portfolio as soon as possible.

The portfolio manager must not rush into a bad investment just to effect matching. Nor is he or she necessarily alone in searching for a suitable means of offsetting the newly acquired instrument(s). Other investment officers within the organization, including those serving on the ALCO, may be able to help. Outside assistance also may be available if the bank has established an ongoing relationship with one or more stable investment houses, brokers, and correspondent banks. Since all of these groups sometimes find themselves in similar situations, they are usually willing to help the portfolio manager obtain the necessary offsetting investments. Further, each stands to make at least a small amount on such a transaction in the form of a fee or a commission. When necessary, then, other investors in the banking industry are almost certain to cooperate with the portfolio manager who is looking for a block of assets or liabilities to add to a bank's holdings.

In most cases, there is time to shop around for the right instrument or block of instruments to offset an investment that has already been made. The bank's position is probably more than stable enough to allow the portfolio manager to spend a few days looking for an offsetting asset or liability that provides a favorable spread. When that item has been found and obtained, the bank wins in at least two ways. First, it stands to make the anticipated profits on the investment that created the imbalance in the first place. Second, with a positive spread between the new investment and the instrument(s) obtained to offset it, additional earnings will be realized on the spread.

In this sense, matched-funding results in positive earnings for banks that accomplish it successfully. Each asset in the portfolio is matched with a liability that has been obtained at a favorable spread. As a result, money earned by the asset is augmented by the earnings on the spread, which causes overall earnings to increase, even if gradually rather than dramatically, further increasing profitability. When this philosophy is applied on a macro basis, with the entire asset side of the portfolio considered in relation to the liability side, the bank assures itself of fairly certain income levels well into the future.

There are no "absolutes." One or more investments may prove to be less desirable than initially anticipated. Also, the positive spread originally determined when an offsetting liability is added sometimes changes and becomes negative (or at least less positive). As noted, some risk always exists in an investment situation. Such factors as unforeseen changes in the overall financial environment, credit failures of parties to large loans, and totally unanticipated swings in interest rates can adversely affect even the best-insulated earnings. With a consistently applied matched funding approach, however, the bank is fairly well insulated against extreme losses on its portfolio.

Long-Range Matched Funding

Matched funding for the longer term can be accomplished gradually. For example, if the gap projections and portfolio analysis indicate that a sizable asset will be renewed six months from now, while the offsetting liability will reprice regardless of that fact, a gradual liability build-up can be effected to accomplish the desired offset. Assume that a large commercial loan is scheduled for payoff in the six-month time bucket, but the borrower has already indicated a preference (and has obtained advance approval) to renew the loan. The offsetting liability, on the other hand, is a block of customer time deposits that, due to projected interest rates, are likely to be withdrawn in that same time frame. What can the bank do to make sure a matched position is maintained?

An obvious step is to start shopping immediately for a single liability, or a group of them, that can be added to the portfolio by that time. If one happens to be available with a maturity that matches that of the asset in question, then the next consideration is whether it can be obtained at a favorable spread. Within these parameters, there is probably sufficient time (six months) for the portfolio manager to procure a suitable liability.

Just in case such a perfectly matched liability cannot be located, however, the bank could take immediate steps to make sure the known asset is matched by the time the existing liability is removed from the portfolio. A concentrated effort might be made to increase consumer time deposits by at least enough to cover the asset in question. Or the bank might decide to emphasize CDs in its promotional efforts, with the objective of adding enough to this segment of the portfolio to offset the asset that is certain to exist. Either way, the bank can establish a point in time at which it evaluates this effort to see if it is attaining the goal. If it is not, enough advance notice should be given to investment personnel to locate the necessary offsetting liability in the open market.

In the above scenario, CDs and time deposits offer the advantage of providing the desired spread, even when variable rates must be paid. These rates can be adjusted (when variable) to assure that at least some favorable spread is maintained between earnings on the asset in question and the interest paid on the liabilities. Further, the incoming funds on customer deposits will be invested, or will be available as needed for the intended purpose of offsetting the asset. In many ways, then, when sufficient advance notice is provided, the "bulk" addition of a liability to offset a known asset (and vice-versa) may be less advantageous than building up to the necessary match by the time it is needed.

Liquidity Considerations

Liquidity, the bank's ability to maintain sufficient sources of funds to meet its financial obligations, must be considered in any portfolio management strategy. If possible, a situation that would require a quick sale of assets at a loss should be avoided. However, there is certainly nothing wrong with a planned liquidation of certain assets to meet obligations as they fall due. These types of asset sales generally do not result in losses and are simply a part of sound investment and portfolio management.

When a bank is actively engaging in matched-funding strategies, special care must be taken that asset sales do not upset the desired balance. Here, perhaps even more than usual, asset sales have far-reaching ramifications. The portfolio manager's efforts to maintain balance between the assets and liabilities in the portfolio can be affected dramatically when the forced sale of assets becomes necessary.

Maintaining the desired (or necessary) liquidity position is an important part of successful portfolio management in every situation and under every approach to investment activities. Adverse liquidity situations that are beyond the portfolio manager's control can sometimes occur. Consideration should be given to off-balance-sheet activity that is possibly not included in the bank's A/L management plans.

Liquidity considerations must be made regardless of the investment strategy employed. These considerations are discussed elsewhere in this book as they relate to those strategies. A portfolio manager who is directed to maintain a generally matched asset and liability stance must be particularly aware of the effects on that position when assets the bank intended to retain must be sold to provide funds in a liquidity crisis.

Summary

A matching policy toward A/L management involves maintaining balance between the interest rate-sensitive assets and liabilities in the investment portfolio. By matching each asset (or major block of assets) with a liability that has essentially the same maturity, rate sensitivity, and liquidity characteristics, the bank can insulate that segment of its investments against significant losses due to changes in market interest rates. This policy may preclude spectacular gains that might be made when rates rise or fall dramatically, but it also helps prevent especially high losses that might otherwise occur due to extreme rate movements.

ASSET/LIABILITY MANAGEMENT TECHNIQUES

Several key factors influence how successfully a bank can maintain a matched position, including:

1. The ability to forecast the gap (difference between rate-sensitive assets and liabilities) that is likely to exist in the portfolio at various future times.
2. The accuracy of the bank's projections of market interest rates in those time frames, plus its recognition of the effects those rates will have on earnings.
3. The ability to manage the gap and keep it at approximately the same (or the desired) level by adding assets or liabilities to, or deleting them from, the portfolio as appropriate.

Gap measurement can be accomplished through the development of profiles and/or the use of simulation modeling. Duration analysis is another measurement technique, and it differs from the others in that it takes the periodic cash flows of assets and liabilities into consideration. Most banks find that a combination of these three methods provides the most accurate projections of the gaps that are likely to exist in their portfolios in various future time frames.

When a bank has more rate-sensitive assets than liabilities in its portfolio, it is said to be in a positive gap position. A balance in favor of rate-sensitive liabilities constitutes a negative gap position. Neither position is necessarily bad or good from an earnings standpoint, because:

- With a positive gap, earnings move in the same direction as interest rates; thus, an upward rate swing means an increase in earnings, and vice-versa.
- In a negative gap situation, earnings move opposite to interest rate movements, which means that an increase in rates results in a decrease in earnings, and vice-versa.

MATCHING TECHNIQUES

If the bank correctly anticipates interest rate fluctuations and establishes a favorable gap position in relation to those fluctuations, earnings will show corresponding increases.

A matched-funding investment policy need not prevent the portfolio manager from taking advantage of opportunities on either the asset or the liability side of the portfolio. Moves to take advantage of outstanding opportunities may temporarily disturb the matched nature of the portfolio, but this imbalance can be corrected in a relatively short time by the addition (or removal) of corresponding investments. This is especially the case when the bank's standing policy is one of matched funding, since the portfolio manager usually has time to effect one or more long-term investments that will offset the move that has been made.

With matching and all other portfolio management techniques, the bank must maintain the necessary liquidity position. Simply defined, liquidity is the bank's ability to meet its obligations as they fall due, without having to sell assets at a loss or take other steps that might be disadvantageous. Appropriate liquidity levels based on sources and uses must be maintained throughout the steps taken to manage the portfolio toward a matched position.

Matching is a conservative approach to investment portfolio management. To many banks, this is a satisfactory position.

2
Swap Techniques

Whether a bank intentionally sets out to establish and maintain a balanced portfolio or simply desires to protect itself against potential interest rate risks by offsetting certain transaction types or volumes with others, several tools and techniques can help accomplish this goal. Among these are contracts in the futures market, options, and interest rate swaps. What these items are and how they work are the subjects of this and the following chapters. The use of these financial tools is then presented in Chapter 5, "Effective Portfolio Management."

As its name implies, a swap is an exchange. Financial swaps differ from most others, however, in one critical detail: A physical exchange of a principal amount never occurs between the parties to a swap. Rather, a *notional* principal is assumed, and net interest payments on that amount are made by one party and received by the other, usually on a regularly scheduled basis. Throughout the lifetime of the swap, the notional principal amount never changes hands.

This type of instrument can be useful to portfolio managers who are trying to manage interest rate risk. For example, if a bank has a large number of floating-rate commercial loans in its portfolio, it may decide to offset the potential interest rate exposure those contracts represent by swapping the floating rate for a fixed rate. It then becomes necessary to locate a counterparty, someone who is willing to exchange fixed-rate interest payments for floating-rate interest payments.

This other party (the counterparty) to the swap may be another bank or financial institution that is trying to offset investments of its own by entering into a swap agreement.

ASSET/LIABILITY MANAGEMENT TECHNIQUES

Or the counterparty may be a speculator who is convinced that there is money to be made by accepting the exchange. In either event, these transactions are conducted in what has become known as the *swap market*.

The swap just described is an interest rate swap, and it is just one of four basic types of swaps that can be used for various purposes. Definitions of all four basic swap structures are in order before this discussion continues.

Types of Swap Structures

The four basic swap structures are:

- *Interest rate swaps*, such as the one in the example, in which one party exchanges a floating interest rate for a fixed rate, or vice-versa.

- *Basis rate swaps*, similar to interest rate swaps except that two floating rates are exchanged, each calculated on a different basis.

- *Fixed-rate currency swaps*, which are exchanges of fixed-rate interest in one currency (the U.S. dollar, for example) for fixed-rate interest in another (perhaps Swiss francs).

- *Currency coupon swaps*, essentially a combination of interest rate and fixed-rate currency swaps in which a fixed rate in one currency is exchanged for a floating rate in another.

Both types of currency swaps may be effected for reasons other than hedging an investment or making an outright profit on the exchange. For example, it is sometimes necessary for a financial institution or a company to obtain funds in a foreign exchange for use in investments in other countries. To obtain sufficient amounts of those foreign funds, one of the currency swaps may prove helpful. For example, if a U.S. corporation intends to build a factory in a developing country in which it is advantageous to pay in a certain foreign currency, a swap for American dollars might provide the necessary funds at a more favorable rate of exchange than is available with a simple conversion of funds to the foreign currency. The availability of the swap market has often made it feasible for such exchanges to occur on a favorable enough basis to proceed with investments that might otherwise have been impractical or impossible.

Currency exchanges and basis rate swaps have become an important part of the world of international finance. While exact figures are difficult to obtain, the total volume of notional principal in the swap market is estimated to exceed $350 billion annually. Large-scale interest rate, base rate, and currency swaps are, in fact, credited with providing a much needed impetus to the world of international finance.

Currency exchanges can become very complicated and are not especially applicable to the typical bank for offsetting potential earnings risks in the portfolio. This is also true of basis rate swaps, which occur mainly in the international marketplace. For most banks, the interest rate swap is the most useful tool for asset/liability management; therefore, this discussion centers on interest rate swaps.

Interest Rate Swaps

An interest rate swap is a transaction in which two parties agree to swap interest payments for a specified period of time. Generally, one of the parties pays a stated, fixed rate of interest, while the counterparty receives a variable rate. Both rates are applied to the established principal amount of the swap. This is called a *notional* principal, however, since it never changes hands. Only the net amount of the interest due to the applicable counterparty is exchanged (Figure 2).

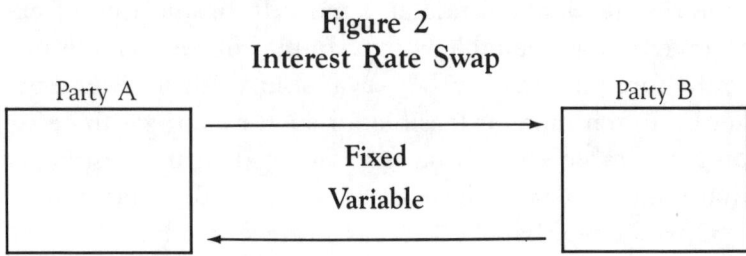

Figure 2
Interest Rate Swap

A swap of the type shown in Figure 2 enables Party A to protect itself against adverse swings in market interest rates by obtaining a long-term commitment from Party B that will partially, if not entirely, offset anticipated exposure risks. This protection is especially important when Party A is funding fixed-rate assets (e.g., loans) and liabilities (e.g., CDs and time deposits). Party B, on the other hand, may need to balance its portfolio by obtaining an assured fixed rate to offset potential exposure resulting from having made several large variable-rate commercial loans. Therefore, Party B is willing to accept the fixed rate offered by Party A, and vice-versa, with the resulting swap protecting both parties against earnings exposure.

Occasionally, one party to a swap is a speculator who thinks that the fixed (or variable) rate offered will result in a profit. This may lead to a certain amount of credit risk for the bank. These risks are discussed later in this chapter. Banks that regularly engage in swaps usually do so through the same channels, thereby minimizing credit risks.

Swaps usually involve large amounts of money, often several hundred million dollars. Minimum swap size is usually a million dollars, however, and this puts the tool well

SWAP TECHNIQUES

within the means of most small banks. A well-designed swap enables a bank to offset potentially dangerous risk positions, as pinpointed by its A/L measurement objectives, by passing at least some of the potential loss on to another party which, for reasons of its own, is willing to accept the exchange of interest payments.

The Costs Involved

When a swap is effected, one party agrees to pay a specified fixed rate on the amount involved. The other party, in turn, agrees to pay a variable rate. This may be LIBOR (the classic free market, or money market, rate), or it may be some other mutually acceptable rate, such as the 30-year Treasury rate. This variable rate (LIBOR) is tied to the spread between market interest rates and the current treasury funds rate, which is determined in London at 11:00 a.m. of each business day. The fixed rate received by one party to the swap is virtually always such that the LIBOR rate returned by the other party is lower. Therefore, when a swap is made, the first party is actually "locking in" to a certain amount of loss (usually relatively low compared to projected potential losses on fixed-rate securities). The party accepting the swap is, at the same time, "locking in" on at least a small profit on its investment.

For example, Party A might agree to pay fixed-rate interest every six months at 7.5%. If the LIBOR returned by Party B averages out at just 6% every six months, the smaller bank is "building in" a loss of 150 basis points on the swap transaction. Party B is not locked in to any specific profit percentage, since the rate it pays is variable. So Party B could make more than originally anticipated if the spread between market and treasury rates moves favorably in relation to its position. The rate charged Party A in this swap is based on

ASSET/LIABILITY MANAGEMENT TECHNIQUES

many years' experience, so it is unlikely that Party B will make significantly less than its anticipated profit.

Before swaps can be used successfully, bank management must adopt a philosophy that makes acceptable the built-in losses that may be involved. Otherwise, the portfolio manager will probably be directed to avoid swaps as a means of controlling the bank's interest rate position. The ALCO is charged with the responsibility of determining when and to what extent swaps can be advantageous to the bank. This involves demonstrating through profiles and model-based projections that, if interest rates move in the anticipated direction, the bank's overall position will be improved, despite the relatively small loss that will automatically be incurred in effecting a swap.

Advantages of Swaps

There are several advantages to swaps which, to many banks, make them well worth the costs. These costs are spread over relatively long terms (two, three, four, even five or more years), and payments are made at regular intervals. The six-month settlement interval used in the examples in this book is typical, although longer and shorter intervals may prevail in given swap situations. Whatever the case, the bank can plan well in advance to meet this interest obligation, since the amount is the same each time (the agreed-upon fixed rate times the total notional principal amount). Further, the party on the receiving end of the more favorable interest payments receives the money regularly, again helping that party in its planning efforts.

Another advantage swaps provide is the ability to use them as a means of funding fixed-rate loans and other transactions. In the past, fixed-rate loan funding was frequently accomplished by issuing fixed-rate CDs. Buyers of these in-

SWAP TECHNIQUES

struments have become increasingly difficult to find, however, since many people feel that variable-rate investments provide them with an opportunity for greater flexibility, especially when short- to medium-term interest rates are volatile. Therefore, swaps have become more prevalent as a means of profitably funding fixed-rate loans.

Swaps can be used to provide an effective hedge against projected interest rate risks. Therefore, they are an effective portfolio management tool when used (and viewed) from the proper perspective. When customer demand, competition, or other factors force a bank to make long-term, fixed-rate loans or accept other fixed-rate instruments, swaps make it possible to minimize the risks of adverse interest rate swings over the maturities of those contracts. Since swaps can be effected without immediate cash outlay, they improve liquidity to the extent that they provide an effective hedge without a capital outlay.

A swap can enable the portfolio manager to create a variable-rate receivable that pays the interest expenses on variable-rate deposits (see Figure 3). The bank pays a fixed rate to the other party in the swap, while receiving a variable (if lower) rate in return. This variable rate received regularly from the other party can be used to pay depositors a variable rate, maintaining a competitive position while minimizing earnings risks in situations in which rising market interest rates are anticipated. The result, in effect, is the conversion of variable-rate deposits to a fixed rate.

There are other ways swaps can be used to the bank's advantage. For example, it may be forced by competitive pressures to accept long term liabilities. If this maturity exceeds the organization's desired limitations, it must find some way to shorten those terms. One way to do this is to locate someone, through the swap market and the brokers

ASSET/LIABILITY MANAGEMENT TECHNIQUES

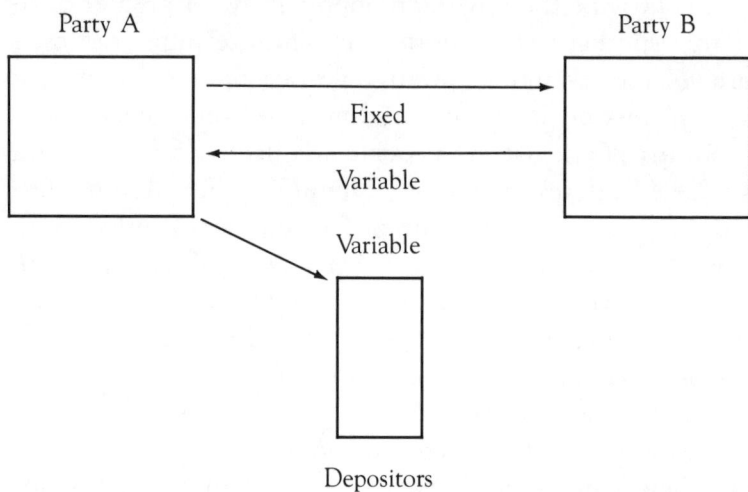

Figure 3
The Variable Rate Received

who handle these transactions, who is willing to swap in exchange for a periodic (six-month, usually) LIBOR. In this instance, one bank is actually *paying* LIBOR to the other party in the swap, a reversal of the roles discussed earlier. This situation requires careful scrutiny and analysis of the LIBOR situation at the given time, but then so does the earlier scenario. If conditions are such that paying the variable-rate LIBOR in exchange for a fixed rate to be paid to the correspondent organization makes sense, then the swap is worth making.

There are occasions when such a favorable situation exists. Suppose, for example, that a bank is able to find three-year money at an attractive variable rate. If someone can be found who is willing to swap securities for a favorable fixed rate, the bank can obtain the available three-year money at the favorable rate, with a net gain in earnings.

But earnings are not the only consideration in this situation, because this is one instance in which a swap can favorably impact the bank's liquidity. The newly acquired three-year funds provide unexpected flexibility in the bank's liquidity position, since it now has more money available for the next three years than anticipated. On occasion then, while swaps in general do not actually "fund" anything and cannot therefore be considered as improving liquidity, this improvement can in fact happen when the bank acquires funds and pays, rather than receives, six-month LIBOR in exchange on a swap.

Finally, having the swap technique available as a balance sheet and portfolio management tool provides a great deal of flexibility to the bank's lending position. In essence, the lending officers have more flexibility to negotiate loan terms, since an ensuing swap can be effected to hedge against an interest rate loss. This does not mean that the usual sound credit practices can be ignored. In fact, credit becomes even more critical than ever when a bank is dealing in swaps, futures, and hedges. It would be difficult (probably impossible) to find willing correspondents in swaps for instruments that were not based on good credit of all parties involved. But in terms of the types of loans, their maturities, and the interest rates and types applicable to them, swaps can be used to provide lending departments with a tremendous amount of flexibility. From this standpoint, commercial, consumer, and mortgage loan departments are likely to appreciate having the swap capability behind them.

Factors in the Swap Decision

Several factors must be considered when deciding whether to enter the swap market. These factors are based largely on the bank's projections of interest rate movements in re-

ASSET/LIABILITY MANAGEMENT TECHNIQUES

lation to its anticipated asset and liability position in various future time frames. The accuracy and comprehensiveness of the bank's gap measurement tools, coupled with its policy toward the investment portfolio and its uses, have a tremendous bearing on whether or not swaps should be considered as a management tool.

Assuming the swap technique is available to the A/L or portfolio manager, here are some of the considerations that must be made:

- *Is the basis risk worth the protection the swap offers?* Both parties to the swap agreement know the fixed rate that is to be paid by one party, so that element of the basis risk is a given. The question is: How much, and in which direction, is the market interest rate likely to move? This factor determines what the other party to the swap returns to the first party at every payment point. If projections indicate that interest rates will rise, the percentage returned to the first party will increase correspondingly, and vice-versa. Again, accurate, timely interest rate projections will help the first party determine whether the swap appears to be worthwhile.

- *What use is to be made of the money received in the swap?* The true cost of these funds to the party paying the fixed rate can be determined as illustrated in Table 2. In this example, the fixed rate charged by the second party to the swap is 7.5%, with a LIBOR (return to the first party) every six months of 6%. The first party pays a net of 1.5% (150 basis points) for the swap. At the same time, the first party must pay its depositors a variable rate that averages 5.5%. This must be added to the fixed cost of 1.5% to get the true net cost of the funds received in the swap—in this case, 7%. If this money can then be invested at a high enough rate, the true cost can be further offset. There can be some tax implications if the invested funds result in a net gain to the bank initiating the swap. (More on this later.) But the true cost of funds usually does not vary significantly, since any increase in LIBOR due to rising rates will be offset by corresponding increases paid to depositors on their variable-rate accounts (see Table 3 for an example of this situation).

Table 2
Typical Net Cost of a Swap

Fixed Rate	7.50%
Six-Month LIBOR	6.00%
Net Paid	1.50%
Cost of Funds*	5.50%
Net Cost	7.00%

*Cost of variable-rate deposits.

Table 3
Market Interest Increases Result in Corresponding Increases in LIBOR

	6 Month	12 Month	18 Month	24 Month
Fixed	(7.0%)	(7.75%)	(7.75%)	(7.75%)
Six-month LIBOR	6.0%	7.0%	8.0%	9.0%
Net Proceeds	(1.75%)	(.75%)	.25%	1.25%
Cost of funds	(5.75%)	(6.75%)	(7.75%)	(8.75%)
Net cost	(7.50%)	(7.50%)	(7.50%)	(7.50%)

Swaps can serve another important function from the macro view when they are used to offset anticipated gap imbalances. The bank must determine, based on its projections of interest rate movements and the size and nature of the anticipated gap, whether the locked-in costs of the swap make it a viable option as compared to other possible actions.

ASSET/LIABILITY MANAGEMENT TECHNIQUES

In making these determinations, the bank must have a firm indication of how various interest rates are moving in relation to each other. Some key relationships between LIBOR, prime, and T-bills are shown in Figure 4. Historically, these rates have paralleled each other fairly closely, but this does not necessarily mean the relationship will remain as stable as it did during 1984, 1985, and the first

Figure 4
Comparison of Prime, Six-Month LIBOR, and 90-Day T-Bill Rates

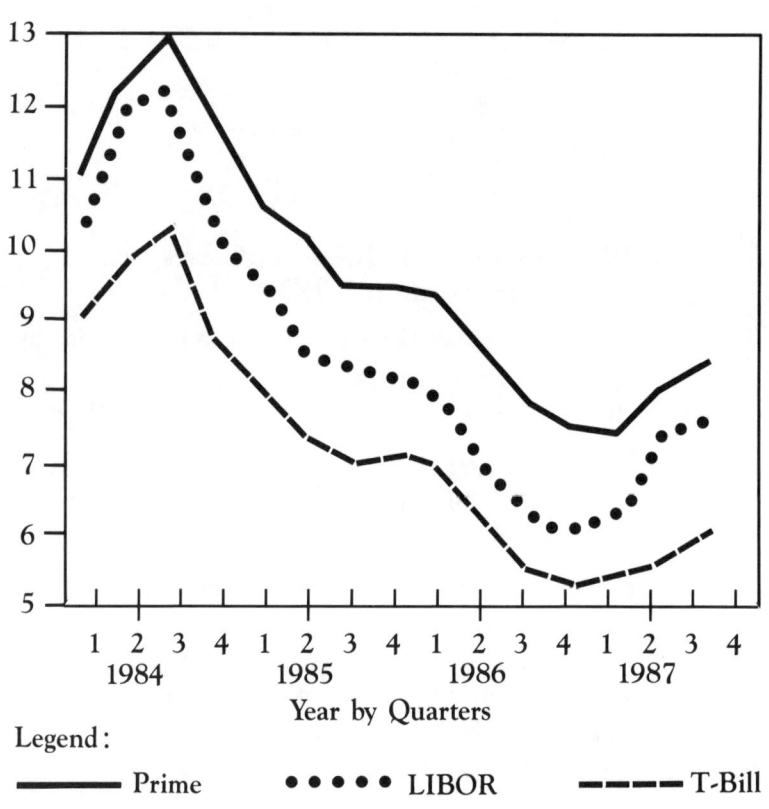

half of 1986. Therefore, the bank should remain constantly aware of day-to-day fluctuations in these relationships, especially since the spread between prime and LIBOR is a good indication of the approximate cost of swaps at any given time.

Swap Implementation

At one time, there was little or no standardization of swaps and how they were implemented. In recent years, however, several of the large money center banks and investment houses that handle such transactions have tried to standardize swap terms to simplify and speed up their consumation. These institutions formed an organization, the International Swap Dealers Association, Inc., and have established a code to follow in implementing swap transactions.[2] The portfolio or A/L manager who is seriously considering using swaps for the first time should review the code at the earliest opportunity.

The subjects covered by the national swap code include such factors as:

- *Cash flow or rate calculations.* This part of the code standardizes the manner in which both the fixed rate paid by the swapping bank, and the variable LIBOR rate paid by the accepting institution are to be determined. In general, the code calls for calculation in the manner discussed earlier: The fixed rate being approximately prime and the variable LIBOR being determined by the current money market (free market) interest rate at the time of payment.

- *Calculation of early termination penalties.* It stands to reason that a bank may find it advantageous to terminate a

---

[2] *Code of Standard Wording, Assumptions and Provisions for Swaps, 1986 Edition.* International Swap Dealers Association, New York, 1986.

ASSET/LIABILITY MANAGEMENT TECHNIQUES

swap agreement before the contractually agreed-upon time. When this occurs, it is only fair for the terminating bank to pay a termination penalty. This is similar in concept to a prepayment penalty on a loan or a lease transaction and is invoked for essentially the same reasons. The originating bank is, in effect, changing the terms of a contract. This forces the other party to make adjustments in its own plans, often at some cost.

Using the guidelines of the swap code, both parties to swaps can now enter into these transactions without individual negotiation. Each knows what is involved when the standard code is used, which reduces tremendously the time required for entering into a swap agreement. *Note, however, that terms of any agreement individually negotiated between the parties to a swap take precedence over the standard terms of the code.* The code is not binding on either party unless it is invoked in the agreement they reach.

In most cases, "invoked" describes how the precepts of the code are used. The bank wishing to make a swap telephones the swap dealer (often a money center bank or investment house) with which it deals and indicates the nature of the desired swap. The accepting bank or company usually indicates in the conversation that the swap agreement—a legal, binding contract on both parties—is to follow specific guidelines of the code. The swap transaction can, in effect, be consummated on the phone, with follow-up by telex and/or formal agreements that make the deal official. Many times, the telex communication is all the swapping bank receives to confirm swaps of up to two years' duration, especially when both parties are well known to each other. Longer swap agreements are usually confirmed by formal contract. By proceeding in this manner, the two parties can agree to and execute a swap in less time than it once took to draw up the agreement, much less obtain the necessary signatures and work out details that almost always followed the same lines.

Development of the national swap code has done more, than just standardize various elements of the agreement. The code has also streamlined the process to the point that swaps are considered very helpful by those portfolio and A/L managers who wish to use them in managing their banks' investments.

The code also recognizes that there may be several viable alternatives for certain aspects of a swap agreement. Therefore, instead of making decisions that only the parties realistically can make at the time an agreement is drawn up, the code offers alternatives the parties can use to state their intentions and obligations. For example, the exact payment intervals can vary, as will the fixed rate charged by the bank accepting the swap. Several other factors can also vary, and by providing the participants with logical alternatives for these factors, the code again facilitates consummation of swap agreements.

The national swap code is not itself a contract or agreement. Rather, it provides guidelines that can be used by reference in specific agreements drawn up by the parties to the individual swap. And, as stated, any contractual stipulations agreed to by the parties to a swap contract override and replace anything in the code that pertains to the same situation. The national swap code is intended to provide standardization to swap contracts where needed and desired by both parties. When the parties have alternatives in mind, their wishes—as written into their own agreement—prevail.

Before a bank enters into the swap market, its attorneys, the A/L manager, the portfolio manager, and any other appropriate people within the organization should review and understand the national swap code. It is to everyone's advantage when references to the code can be made in individual swap agreements. This saves time, which translates to money, and enables both parties to enter these agreements with the same ground rules in mind.

Credit Considerations in Swap Transactions

The national swap code does not address credit issues. Sound credit practices dictate that each party to the swap must be certain of the other's good credit. However, if the originating bank is using the swap to hedge a block of loans, then that bank must be especially careful to do a thorough job of credit investigation and evaluation on the parties to those loans.

Credit judgment (or a lack of it) by one bank soon becomes apparent to correspondents. If a bank has established a good reputation for being attentive to its loan customers' credit capabilities and performances, other organizations come to trust its judgment. This makes a money center bank or an investment house more willing to accept swaps, sometimes at interest rates that are more favorable than they might be if the bank had a poor credit evaluation record. Banks engaging in swaps are usually "known quantities" in terms of credit judgments, which is one reason why nothing is (or need be) stated in the national swap code.

If a bank is new to the swap market or has a reputation of being less than sound in its credit judgments when making loans, the money center bank or investment house may require more stringent credit actions than are specified in the clauses of the national swap code. The institution being asked to accept the swap may require the bank to pay a higher fixed rate than usual. Or it may penalize the bank a few basis points on the LIBOR rate returned on at least the first few payment dates. If sound credit judgments are generally practiced by the bank wanting to implement a swap, the standard credit requirements should prevail.

If an institution other than a large money center bank or substantial investment house becomes involved in a swap transaction, the A/L or portfolio manager must try to determine who those additional parties are. For example, if a relatively large bank (although not considered a money center bank) accepts a swap, it may decide to pass the transaction on to another financial institution or investor. There may, in fact, be more than one such organization involved, especially if the swap is quite large. A savings and loan may accept some of the swap from the large bank; and part of it may be passed on to another, smaller bank, an investment company, or even a broker for further dissemination. This is beyond the initial bank's control unless stipulations preventing these actions are included in the swap agreement.

The validity of a swap depends heavily on each party's ability and willingness to live up to its end of the bargain. If one party reneges, for whatever reason, then the agreement becomes invalid. There is legal recourse, obviously, since the swap agreement is a legal, binding contract. However, it is far better to do an initial careful credit check than to have to resort to such action to enforce the terms of a contract. A serious problem can exist when the initiating bank is unaware that the bank or other institution accepting the swap intends to pass it along to others. The originator may not be able personally to determine what other parties are involved, much less do any sort of credit check on them. This is where the A/L or portfolio manager would be well advised to call on the bank's credit staff to help with the situation.

ASSET/LIABILITY MANAGEMENT TECHNIQUES

Credit checks can be conducted on virtually any individual or organization, if the problem is properly approached and handled. In every bank, there are experts whose primary expertise lies in performing such tasks on a daily basis. The individual in charge of instituting swap transactions should not hesitate to ask his own bank's experts for assistance. They can follow up to make sure all parties who are going to be involved down the line have the capacity and the proven willingness to perform as expected.

Initially, at least, the investments manager should confine swap activities to agreements involving established banks and investment houses. These organizations are accustomed to handling swaps and tend to deal only with other banks and companies that have proven credit standings. Later, when the A/L or portfolio manager has gained experience in dealing with various parties in placing (perhaps even accepting) swaps, it may be possible to work with smaller correspondent banks and investors.

In no case, however, should credit factors be ignored in placing and/or accepting swaps. These transactions usually involve large sums of money and, therefore, sizable fixed-rate and LIBOR payments at each designated date. A small- or medium-sized bank's earnings position can be dealt a serious blow if just one payment is missed or not made on a timely basis. The default penalties written into most swap contracts offer some degree of protection. But when an inability to pay exists, these contract clauses are worth no more than any other defaulted contract. Careful credit decisions prior to signing swap contracts are always advised, especially since most banks have in-house expertise in these matters.

These credit evaluations also apply to any brokers who may be involved in swap transactions for the bank. If possible, their financial statements should be reviewed, and their operations should be checked out through the usual credit sources (Dun & Bradstreet or the local credit bureau, for example, depending on the bank's policy). Again, the people best qualified to handle such matters are the bank's own credit experts.

Credit risks exist in a swap when one party to the agreement defaults. Since no principal amount has changed hands, however, the extent of the actual interest rate risk will be no worse than it was before the swap transaction was instituted. This exposure decreases as time passes and net interest payments are exchanged, so the longer the swap remains in effect without either party's defaulting, the lower the risk becomes. There may be some replacement costs if the initiating party wishes to replace a swap on which the other party has defaulted, especially if less favorable rates must be accepted to establish a new swap. Still, credit risks are usually minimal with swaps when both parties are known factors. This makes these transactions even more attractive to the manager who wants to create flexibility for the bank's overall investment effort while simultaneously obtaining interest rate risk protection for the portfolio.

Measuring Interest Rate Risk Exposure in Swaps

Because one party to an interest rate swap receives a variable rate and the other a fixed rate, there is always a certain amount of interest rate risk in swap transactions. The A/L, portfolio, or investments manager must have some means of calculating the extent of that exposure. Two basic approaches have proven successful: the projection method, and the use of a formula. The following discussions explain how to use these approaches.

ASSET/LIABILITY MANAGEMENT TECHNIQUES

The Projection Approach

The projection approach to determining the interest rate risk presented by a swap involves *estimating the cost of an offsetting position*—what it would take, and at what expense, to offset the swap(s) should unfavorable interest rate shifts cause them to cost more than anticipated. This approach only works when a bank is active enough in the swap market to be constantly updating its swap position. A bank that is relatively inactive in the swap market will probably find that the time and effort required to make accurate projections probably make the technique impractical. The amount of information that can be put into projections in these cases results in sketchy, often inaccurate results.

The same kinds of techniques that are used to estimate gap projections and earnings risks can be used to estimate the costs involved in establishing an offsetting position to potentially adverse swaps. Profiles that extend well into the future are necessary for this purpose, since swap terms are often as long as five years. Computer models are helpful in calculating the risk presented by a swap because so many variables must be considered.

To establish an offsetting position, the bank must buy or sell specific securities, increase deposits, arrange for money to be available on relatively short notice, perhaps even engage in additional swaps that provide the opposite effects of those already booked—whatever it takes to make certain that the bank will be protected adequately if rates reach a point at which the LIBOR the bank receives is less than the fixed rate paid to the other bank or investment company.

In addition to the many different types of securities or other investments that might be made, the estimate must include scenarios depicting various potential interest rate conditions over the period of the swap. All these variables are difficult to project and calculate.

The Formula Approach

A much simpler means of determining interest rate risks presented by swaps is to apply the following formula to the swap(s) in question:

$$\text{Par Value} \times 3\% \times \text{Years to Swap Maturity}$$

Par value is the stated nominal value on which the interest payment exchange of a swap is based. While this amount is never actually exchanged, it is the amount to which both the floating and the fixed interest rates are applied in calculating the net payments between the two parties.

The three percent by which the par value is multiplied represents an estimate of the exposure presented by the swap. It is representative of the difference between the fixed rate paid by one party and the variable rate that party receives (or is likely to receive) over the life of the swap. The actual difference may be more or less than three percent, but this rate is currently used as a standard for interest rate exposure calculations in swaps. Initially, five percent was used as the multiplier in the formula; then four percent became the standard as greater experience was gained in the swap market. Even longer experience has resulted in the use of three percent, although the figure still ranges from three to four percent in some banks' calculations.

Since the formula can be applied to the total notional principal of outstanding swaps whenever desired, the amount at risk can be calculated at any time. But on any given swap, the amount of exposure decreases with each year's passage of time. This is depicted in Table 4, in which the amount of interest rate risk decreases steadily over the five-year maturity of a $10 million swap.

47

ASSET/LIABILITY MANAGEMENT TECHNIQUES

Because of its relative simplicity, many banks find the formula approach to measuring interest rate risks of swaps more appealing than the projection approach. Projection of these risks in all the potential scenarios is relatively complicated. Banks that are already using sophisticated, automated interest rate and gap projection methods, however, may find that the greater accuracy and flexibility provided by the projection approach is worthwhile.

Table 4
Interest Rate Risk Exposure
Five-Year Swap
$10,000,000 Par Value

Year 1:	$10,000,000	(.03)	5 Years	=	$1,500,000
Year 2:	$10,000,000	(.03)	4 Years	=	1,200,000
Year 3:	$10,000,000	(.03)	3 Years	=	900,000
Year 4:	$10,000,000	(0.3)	2 Years	=	600,000
Year 5:	$10,000,000	(0.3)	1 Year	=	300,000

Accounting for Swaps

A swap is an off-balance sheet item that must be accounted for. The exact method of swap accounting has not yet been formulated in the industry's generally accepted accounting principles (GAAP), although such standards may soon be forthcoming. Since these guidelines are yet to be prepared, a commonsense approach to swap accounting is recommended.

One of the following approaches should be sufficient for swap accounting until the appropriate GAAP guidelines are published:

- *Settlement accounting.* Footnotes should be made in the bank's financial statements to acknowledge the existence of the swap transactions and to inform investors that the institution is engaging in swaps. The net payments involved in each swap are recorded in the period in which they are due, which means that no accounting, other than the footnotes, would be done until payment is received or made, as appropriate to the transaction. This is the method most accountants prefer when the swap can be linked to an existing liability. It helps avoid unanticipated income adjustments resulting from interest rate changes that affect the value of the swap.

- *Mark-to-market method.* This approach makes it possible to account for increases or decreases in the value of the swap agreement as interest rates fluctuate. These changes in value are accounted for as they occur instead of waiting for the net change that prevails in the period in which the cash is exchanged per the agreement. Either this or the unrealized loss method (below) is recommended by accountants when no distinct link can be established between the swap and a particular asset or liability.

- *Unrealized loss accounting.* This method works just like the mark-to-market approach, except only losses in the value of the swap transaction are recorded in the period incurred. Further, if a loss was recorded previously but has now been reversed, any recovery of that previously recorded loss is recorded under this system.

As noted, most accountants recommend mark-to-market or unrealized loss accounting for swap values when a distinct link can be established between the swap and a particular asset or liability. These approaches take the view that swaps are speculative, at least to the extent that fluctuating interest rates can affect their values. With all three approaches, however, it is recommended that footnotes be used to disclose the bank's swap activity, even if accounting for the net interest exchanges is left until the periods in which these exchanges actually occur.

Although disclosure is extremely important, until generally accepted accounting principles are formulated and published, the decision as to how to account for swap transactions is left to the bank's discretion.

Variations on the Theme

The discussion in this chapter has centered on the basic swap most commonly used by banks to protect earnings against interest rate exposure presented by the items in their portfolios. There can be some variations on this basic theme, however, including swaps which:

- *Pay variable, receive variable rates.* This common agreement has the initiating bank paying a six-month LIBOR and receiving the Treasury rate in return. The results are essentially the same as with a conventional swap since, as shown in Figure 4, the relationship between prime, LIBOR, and treasury rates historically remains fairly constant.

- *Offer deferred takedown and deferred rate-setting.* Both of these types of swaps are used primarily in the real estate business and are not especially applicable to banking situations.

- *Involve cross-currency agreements.* These swaps can result in trading instruments (and payments) in the currencies of different nations. For example, Eurodollars involved in one security, or group of securities, are swapped for transactions made with U.S. dollars. Cross-currency swaps enable a bank to take advantage of currency value differences to put itself in a better position.

There may be other variations in swap contracts, depending on the needs and wishes of the parties involved. The degree to which swaps are used in a given bank depends on its investment philosophy and how far it wants to go in manipulating its portfolio. The A/L, portfolio, or investments manager must be aware of what these tools are and how they work, because they can be important in the effort to establish and maintain the desired position for the bank.

Summary

Swaps can be extremely useful to the A/L manager, the portfolio manager, and other parties who are responsible for helping establish and maintain a bank's earnings position through asset/liability management. A swap allows the bank to exchange interest rates with another party. One party may want to lock in a fixed interest rate over a specified period, and another may want a variable rate. This activity can be accomplished without affecting access to capital markets for additional fixed-rate funding, since a swap is an exchange of interest payments and, as such, does not involve principal amounts. Because no principal changes hands, the parties agree to a notional amount on which interest payments are made.

Once a bank has established itself in the swap market, these transactions can be conducted with minimal delay and documentation. Most swaps between established parties are handled by telephone, with a simple follow-up telex or similar document spelling out the particulars of the agreement. This is made possible, in part, by general adoption and acceptance of the national swap code, which sets forth basic clauses that can be incorporated into a given swap agreement by reference. The code provides logical alternatives for situations requiring them, further simplifying the process of working out an agreement that is acceptable to both parties.

The code is not the swap agreement itself, however; it simply provides the parties to the contract with a standard set of clauses that can be adopted "as is," or varied to fit the situation. The exact terms of the swap agreement to which both parties agree take precedence over the standard clauses, because they are the statements that comprise the swap contract itself.

With swap capability, bank loan departments can accommodate new or present customers who require fixed-rate loans. These transactions can be accepted, then backed by a swap to protect the bank's earnings position against adverse variations in market interest rates. And since a swap can provide fixed-rate money, the bank may find itself paying a rate that is below that available on the general market.

Each bank that intends to enter the swap market needs a stated policy to this effect. Once the statement is in position, it is up to the ALCO, including the portfolio and/or investments manager, to use swaps to advantage to protect the bank's earnings position. This means the responsible parties must keep themselves fully aware of interest rate positions and relationships (prime, T-bill, and LIBOR) at all times so swaps can be used to optimize the bank's position under whatever conditions exist.

Swaps represent an important tool in almost any bank's portfolio and investment management efforts. Combined with good overall management techniques and some of the other sophisticated tools available, including futures and options, swaps make it possible to remain competitive without incurring excessive risks.

3
Futures as a Hedging Technique

A futures contract is a commitment to deliver or accept an item at a stated price and on a specified future date. For centuries, futures were used in the agricultural market, providing a means of both hedging and price discovery for the entire industry. In recent years, agricultural futures have been traded through exchanges, such as the Chicago Mercantile Exchange (CME). It was this exchange which, in 1972, was instrumental in developing and introducing the first financial futures contracts.

The CME applied the concepts that had long been used in the agricultural industry—contracts that guaranteed delivery and acceptance of specific items on specified dates and at stated prices—to the exchange of foreign currencies. For example, through brokers who had access to the exchange, two parties could agree to trade U.S. dollars for Swiss francs at some future date and at an exchange rate agreed upon at contract inception. Such an agreement enabled one party to "lock in" the costs of obtaining one type of currency, thereby hedging against increases in the costs of those funds. Simultaneously, the other party, anticipating that the exchange rate would be favorable to it on the specified date, would enter into the agreement to deliver the specified currency at the contract price.

These *forward* agreements worked so well that they were soon expanded to include similar contracts on various types of financial instruments, not just currencies. Today, futures contracts are even available based on projected stock price indexes (the Standard & Poor's 500 Index, for example); and

53

the total daily futures market for all commodities, currencies, and financial instruments regularly amounts to hundreds of billions of dollars.

For the asset/liability manager, futures contracts involving financial instruments can represent an important risk management tool. This chapter explains these contracts and how they can be used to hedge against earnings risks in portfolio management.

Forwards

A futures contract is generally classified as a type of forward, which is a contract in which two parties agree to exchange a specified item (or items) on a certain date in the future. The quantity of the item, the price, and the maturity date (exchange date) are specified at contract inception. Forwards are not generally traded on an exchange. The contract changes hands directly between the two parties involved or through an intermediary, such as a commercial or investment bank. Settlement of the contract usually occurs upon maturity, with no additional action by either party in the interim.

There is no standard contract form for forwards. Instead, each agreement is customized to meet the needs of the parties involved. In a foreign currency forward, one party agrees to exchange one currency for another, with delivery to occur at a specified future date. This is as opposed to a "spot" currency trade, in which one currency is exchanged for another on-the-spot (in reality, within two days, since it may take that long for the necessary amount of currency to become deliverable from foreign markets). A bank or company that anticipates a need for funds in a foreign currency might opt to buy that currency on-the-spot market (today),

FUTURES AS A HEDGING TECHNIQUE

or on a forward basis, depending on how it views current and future exchange rates.

Differences in exchange rates are actually reflections of the interest rates that can be obtained on investments in each of the currencies. When interest rates go up, that attracts foreign investment; the economy is stronger, and exchange rates are stronger, making them less attractive to foreigners. The party with the anticipated need for foreign funds may expect the foreign interest rate to fall and decide that it is to its advantage simply to buy currency at today's spot market exchange rate. If that party feels that a more favorable rate of exchange may be realized at a future date, however, it may decide to enter into a currency forward agreement with another party who has the opposite view or is hedging a different position.

Interest rate forwards are also available. These are agreements to deliver, at specified prices and on specified dates, various interest rate-sensitive instruments. Since there is no standard forward contract, the terms of such forwards, including instrument types, prices, rates, and delivery dates, are established by the parties to the agreement on whatever basis is satisfactory to both. Because interest rate forwards are relatively sophisticated, with both parties negotiating the terms of the agreement instead of operating under a standard contract, these instruments are not used as often as swaps, futures, and options in asset/liability management. This situation may change, however, as increasingly sophisticated financial instruments (and the need to hedge the risks they present) are developed.

Futures as Types of Forwards

Futures contracts are generally classified as a type of forward, but there are some important differences that have

ASSET/LIABILITY MANAGEMENT TECHNIQUES

helped make futures more widely used in A/L management. These differences are:

1. *Futures contracts are exchange-traded.* This results in the presence of a viable, liquid marketplace, with the exchange acting as a principal to every futures transaction. The parties wishing to engage in futures contracts work through brokers who, in turn, pass the offerings through the exchange. This process adds stability and liquidity to the futures market. It also makes it possible to obtain prices on contemplated contracts before actually offering them, since brokers in these instruments stay aware of the futures that are being bought and sold at all times.

2. *Futures contracts are standardized.* Only certain types of contracts can be bought and sold through the exchange. This simplifies matters for the portfolio or asset/liability manager, since most of the details of the contract, including quantities and delivery dates, are pre-established. The variable element of a futures contract is its price, and with the availability of quotes, the manager can determine whether a given sale or purchase on the futures market is likely to be advantageous.

3. *Cash settlements, based on the market value of each position, are made daily*, rather than as a single settlement upon contract maturity. This feature, especially, distinguishes futures contracts from other types of forwards.

Futures contracts are forwards in that they specify transaction terms that pertain to some point in the future. They are different from other forwards, however, in the important ways noted here. How important these differences are will become increasingly apparent as this discussion progresses.

How Futures Work

To use futures effectively, the portfolio or A/L manager must have a thorough understanding of how they work. First, the meanings of the terms *long* and *short* must be redefined, since they have a different meaning in regard to futures contracts than in other contexts. A party to a futures contract who agrees to take delivery of the financial instruments involved is said to be in a *long* position. Conversely, the party who agrees to make delivery is said to be in a *short* position.

While a futures contract specifies the terms of delivery of the underlying financial instruments, in most cases, neither party *expects* to make or accept delivery of those instruments. The vast majority of futures contracts are settled in cash before the delivery date, usually by execution of another futures contract that takes the opposite position from the one taken initially. This is logical, since the objective of a futures contract (for the A/L manager, although not necessarily for the futures speculator) is to hedge a risk position with an offsetting investment. And since investment portfolios are constantly changing, so are the bank's hedging requirements. It stands to reason that the least costly method of satisfying a long or short futures contract position is to offset it with an opposite position prior to maturity.

This manipulation of positions can be accomplished with relatively little actual cash outlay due to the nature of the futures market (see Figure 5). If Party A decides it is advantageous to assume a short position, that is, to deliver a specific financial instrument at a certain price and on a given date in the future, it contacts its broker and makes its wishes known. The broker then checks the exchange to determine

ASSET/LIABILITY MANAGEMENT TECHNIQUES

the availability of an appropriate futures contract. In the meantime, another party (Party B, for this discussion) has contacted its broker, who in turn has checked with the exchange, in search of a position opposite to the one sought by Party A. Through the exchange, then, the two parties' brokers arrange the necessary futures contract.

Figure 5
Elements of a Futures Contract

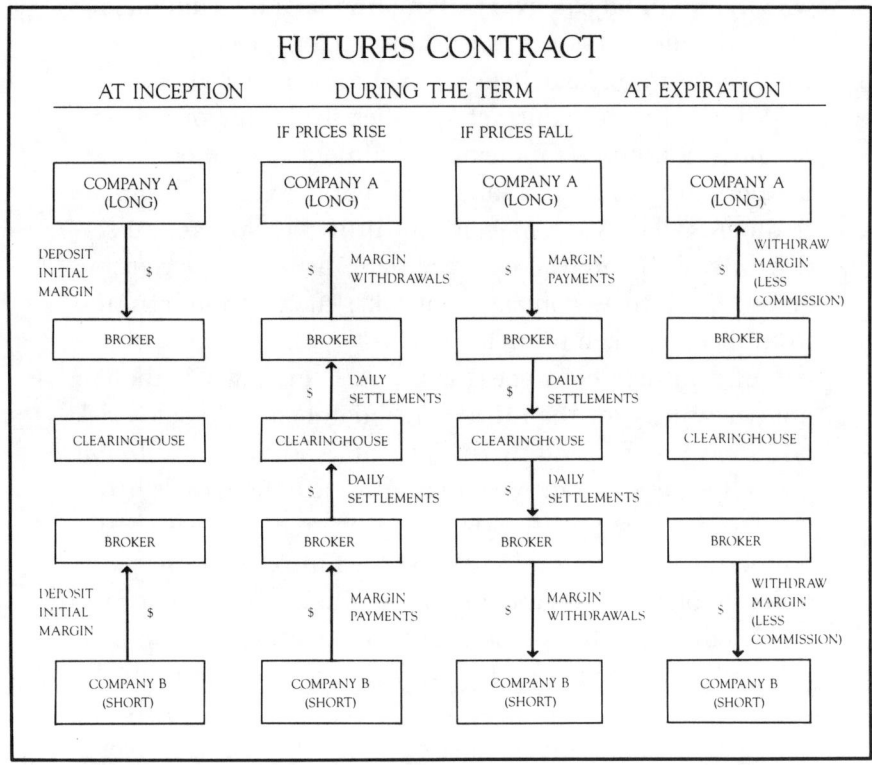

Reprinted with permission of Price Waterhouse from *Hedging: Foreign Exchange and Interest Rate Risk Management Implementation Guide*. Copyright © 1986 Price Waterhouse. All rights reserved.

FUTURES AS A HEDGING TECHNIQUE

At contract inception, both parties deposit initial margin amounts with their brokers. Neither is required to pay the entire amount of the contract, just the initial margin requirements. These can be surprisingly low (as little as 0.1 percent of the face amount, for example, on some futures contracts). Further, the broker's fees are also quite low due to competition in the marketplace, so both parties can establish their desired long and short positions with very little actual cash outlay.

The brokers are responsible for settling their accounts with the exchange at the end of each business day. The daily closing price of each futures contract is used to determine the broker's standing. If there has been a net decrease in the market value of all open futures positions held by the broker, they must pay the exchange an amount equal to that net decrease. Conversely, they receive daily payment from the exchange for the amount of any net increase in their total futures positions.

The broker then credits (or charges) their individual futures customers for their shares of amounts received from (or amounts the broker must pay to) the exchange. These debits and credits to individual futures customers' accounts are called *variation margins*. Customers whose accounts increase above the ongoing margin amount required by the broker (the *maintenance margin*) can withdraw the excess amount in cash. Similarly, if losses draw the customer's margin account below the maintenance margin, the broker places a margin call requiring the customer to submit enough cash (or government securities) to make up the difference.

Brokers' fees on futures contracts are based on commissions, but they are determined on the basis of "round turns" (both the opening and closing transactions), since every futures contract will be closed, one way or another—usually

ASSET/LIABILITY MANAGEMENT TECHNIQUES

by establishing an opposing futures position as noted earlier. Because futures require only margin payments rather than payments of face amounts, they can be used effectively to hedge a portfolio manager's risks while making it possible to conserve the bank's funds for investment purposes or to meet liquidity needs.

Interest Rates on Futures Contracts

Whether a party to a futures contract is establishing a long position (agreeing to take delivery) or a short position (contracting to deliver), the interest rate on the transaction is established at the time the contract is made. This rate establishment can be in the form of either a ceiling or a floor, instead of a specific rate. Essentially, however, a futures contract, like a swap, enables one party to hedge variable-rate instruments with what amounts to a fixed rate in a futures contract, or vice-versa.

If one party buys a futures contract and interest rates increase, that party has foregone the potential to earn that higher rate. The seller is contractually bound to sell at the established rate, even though a greater profit could be realized by selling elsewhere. This potential loss of increased interest earnings should rates rise represents the true cost of this hedge. On the other hand, if rates have decreased, a loss that might otherwise have been incurred is prevented due to the fixed-rate nature of the futures contract.

A futures contract might call for a range of rates (called ceilings and floors), instead of just a single fixed rate. For example, the fixed rate might be established at 9%, and if the market rate on the maturity date is actually 10%, the hedger cannot profit from the improved rate picture—they are bound to the 9% arrangement called for in the contract. But if the contract sets a ceiling of 10% and a floor of 8%, the hedger can earn up to the 10% ceiling. If the actual rate is 11% on the contract maturity date, the hedger cannot make that full rate; but does receive up to the established ceiling of 10%. Conversely, a floor written into the agreement minimizes the loss. If the prevailing rate on the maturity date is 7%, the hedger is still guaranteed 8% (the floor) thus minimizing the loss.

Futures are gaining increasing acceptance as an asset/liability management tool, since they provide the portfolio manager with access to an additional market that can help in the effort to maintain and protect the bank's position. Futures contracts represent a viable means of hedging against adverse fluctuations in market interest rates.

Characteristics of Futures Contracts

How futures can be used to protect the bank's position against potential interest rate (earnings) risks is more easily recognized when the characteristics of futures contracts are understood. The following discussion explains how contracts are standardized and are structured to help the parties protect their liquidity positions, as well as provide a hedge against adverse interest rate fluctuations.

Standardized Contracts

Several factors in futures contracts have been standardized to make them easy to use. Among the standardized items are:
- *Dollar amounts*. Futures contracts have face amounts of $1 million. More than one contract can be used when greater amounts are needed.
- *Underlying instruments*. These are usually Eurodollars, Treasury bills, T-bonds, or foreign currency. These in-

struments all have a similar underlying characteristic: Their prices fluctuate with changes in interest rates.

- *Underlying instrument maturity.* The maturity terms of the Eurodollars, T-bills, and T-bonds used as the underlying instruments for futures contracts are always quarterly. These dates follow calendar quarters, so the instruments mature in March, June, September, and December. The bank that deals in futures contracts, then, knows both the types of instruments involved and their maturity dates. Further, since the usual contract increment is $1 million, even the face amount is known. These known quantities help simplify transactions in the futures market, resulting in fast, timely decisions and equally efficient execution of transactions once decisions have been made.

- *Delivery and expiration dates.* Since the maturities of the instruments are known in advance, the bank knows exactly when it must be prepared to pay for futures contracts purchased and when it will receive its money for contracts sold. Again, this simplifies the use of futures as portfolio management tools. Much of the uncertainty as to when to buy or sell is removed. These factors are all decided by the nature of the futures contract, so if the bank finds itself in an adverse position at any point during the contract, it has a specific deadline by which offsetting action must be taken.

This standardization of the futures contract has helped increase its popularity as a portfolio management tool.

Liquidity

Futures contracts offer a highly liquid method of managing interest rates. If a bank buys a futures contract, then

FUTURES AS A HEDGING TECHNIQUE

finds itself facing an unexpected liquidity requirement, it is usually easy to find a buyer for the contract at a reasonable rate. Futures are short-term contracts, usually 90-day and seldom ranging beyond a year in maturity. Even if the bank faces a period of unexpectedly tight liquidity, it often is possible to wait until the end of the contract to sell as originally planned, since contract maturity is never all that far into the future. Futures contracts that extend beyond 12 months tend to lose their liquidity advantage. By that time, they are considered low-quality paper with relatively low resale value. But within the framework of 90-day contracts, or a series maturing within the coming year, they provide greater liquidity than do many other types of hedging transactions.

Flexibility and Ease of Use

Since futures contract buyers and sellers all work through the same exchange in the United States (the Chicago Board of Trade), the bank can easily adjust its position by buying or selling a contract that provides an offsetting position, if necessary. Once a position is established with the Board of Trade, all the bank has to do is notify the appropriate floor trader on the exchange (usually through its broker) to effect the sale or purchase of a futures contract. This enables the bank to remain flexible in its efforts to establish and maintain a desired asset/liability position. There are usually some expenses involved in deciding to terminate a futures contract early, but these charges may be insignificant if a bank discovers that it must suddenly adjust its position to avoid an adverse situation. With futures contracts, adjustments can be made on very short notice.

Low Cost

Fees charged by the exchange and brokers for handling futures transactions have remained low, especially in comparison to broker and other charges involved in such transactions as stock sales and purchases. This fact makes futures a cost-effective investment management technique.

The standardized nature of the futures contract has helped it gain in popularity in recent years. The portfolio managers who have this tool at their disposal know they can use futures to their advantage without having to worry about many factors that are always of concern with other types of management tools. They know what they are buying or selling, what the underlying instruments are, when the contracts will mature, and what their costs will be upon contract maturity. These standard factors, coupled with the flexibility and liquidity these contracts offer, help make futures contracts useful.

Futures Versus Swaps

At first glance, futures contracts and swaps might appear to be the same. Both are used to accomplish much the same objective, since each provides a means of hedging against potentially adverse fluctuations in market interest rates. Both swaps and futures are considered to be symmetric types of hedges because they enable the hedger to transfer financial risk, thereby balancing out (making symmetrical) earnings risks due to market interest rate fluctuations. But swaps are generally used to establish longer-term hedges, while futures can work effectively in the shorter term—often as little as 90 days, since the futures market deals primarily in 90-day contracts.

There are other critical differences between swaps and futures contracts, including:

FUTURES AS A HEDGING TECHNIQUE

- Swaps may involve almost any type of instrument, as long as another party who is willing to make the trade can be found. Futures contracts usually involve specific types of underlying instruments—Eurodollars, Treasury bills, Treasury bonds, or foreign currency.
- Swaps can be effected on the open market and need not be conducted through a specified exchange. An independent broker can handle them without going through any exchange, in fact, if the broker knows of a correspondent who is willing to accept the proposed swap. Futures contracts, on the other hand, are conducted through a specific exchange (in the United States, the Chicago Board of Trade) and are much more standardized in terms of underlying instruments (the three mentioned above), maturity dates of those instruments, and the maturity or expiration date of each contract.
- Swaps involve no initial outlay of cash, since only interest payments are exchanged. With futures, the initial margin amount must be provided to the broker (usually in cash or government securities), so there is at least that amount of immediate cash outlay. In addition, margin calls may require additional payments to the broker, although these may be offset over time if the hedger is able to make margin withdrawals as a result of favorable price swings in daily contract settlements.

An important difference between futures contracts and swaps lies in the long- or short-term nature of the instrument(s) being hedged. Swaps generally represent much longer-term hedges, while futures contracts are generally for the shorter term. As a result, futures offer greater liquidity possibilities. Funds are tied up for shorter periods, and it

ASSET/LIABILITY MANAGEMENT TECHNIQUES

is often easier to find another party to take over the contract. This can become costly in terms of net earnings or losses on futures contracts; but should a liquidity "crunch" occur, the ability to obtain funds on short notice sometimes makes these contracts more appealing than swaps.

Basis and Basis Risk

The concepts of basis and basis risk must be understood before attempting to use futures as an interest rate risk hedging mechanism. Simply stated:

$$\text{Basis} = \text{Cash Price} - \text{Futures Price}$$

Hedging using the futures market is accomplished by managing the basis position, that is, keeping the difference between the cash price of an instrument (or group of instruments) and the futures price within a favorable or desirable range. Once the portfolio manager begins using futures, he or she must be concerned with basis risk, along with the usual interest rate risk considerations.

Actually, interest rate and basis risk concerns are inseparable, since the interest rate yield curve drives basis (see Figure 6). The cash price of an investment is what it costs to purchase it as of the moment. The future price for that same investment (instrument) may be higher or lower than today's cash price, and this has a direct bearing on whether a particular futures contract makes sense in a given bank's A/L management plan. A higher or a lower future price may be preferred, depending on the bank's objectives and its overall position both now and at the projected future date. While the terms *investment* and *instrument* are used in singular form in this discussion, the concepts presented may and often do apply to an entire group of individual instruments that are

Figure 6
Financial Futures—Basis*

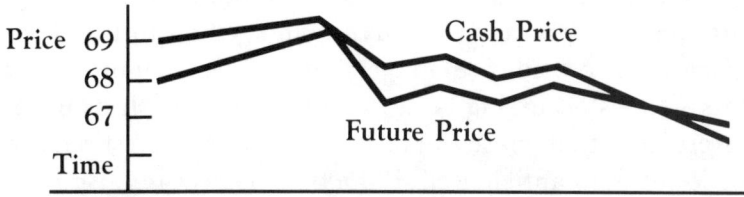

†Basis—the difference between cash and future prices of an instrument—follows the lower curve if cash and future prices vary as illustrated in the upper curve comparison.

pulled together to form a single investment whose risks are to be offset by futures market activities.

Basis *points* are established as hundredths of a percentage point. In other words, a movement in interest rates of 1% is a move of 100 basis points. A 1.5% change is 150 basis points, and so on. Further, the futures contract has been standardized so that, on an investment of $1 million in the futures market, each basis point is worth $25. Thus, a change in interest of one full percentage point makes a difference of $2,500 ($25 x 100 basis points) on each $1 million futures contract. This standardization of values adds to the attractiveness of the futures market for many investors, because they can readily calculate their losses or gains at any given point by determining the change in basis points (up or down) and multiplying by the standard $25 figure.

Hedging in the futures market is tantamount to managing the basis position. By buying and selling futures contracts, the portfolio manager can protect against basis loss—losses occurring because of unfavorable shifts in interest rates that cause the future price of an investment to be lower than anticipated. If the bank is hedging using futures, then management of basis, which is driven by the interest-based yield curve, also results in management of interest rate risk.

For example, if a bank owns a bond, it is exposed to any unfavorable movement in the outright price of that instrument. If interest rates increase prior to the maturity date of the bond, the bank may have to sell it at a lower price. To protect itself against this potential loss in the price of the bond, the bank might decide to establish a futures position—in this instance, sell a futures contract—that will offset the potential loss on the bond. Once this future is sold, a basis has been created. In short, a difference has been created between today's cash price of the bond and the projected future price of that instrument.

Historically, basis spread has been less volatile than cash prices on instruments such as bonds. If basis were not more stable over a period of time, then no hedging position or vehicle could exist. Generally, cash and futures prices move together, while basis remains more stable. This characteristic is what makes it possible to hedge potential cash losses on an instrument with a futures contract. For this hedge to work, the basis must be at the proper level when the contract is obtained. From there, it must be managed properly to retain the advantages that should be forthcoming from the hedge and to protect the bank's earnings position.

The importance of tracking basis is obvious, since the hedger who is aware of and recognizes peaks and valleys in the basis spread can buy or sell futures contracts at points that provide a bank with the greatest advantage. For example, if the spread between the cash price and the future price of a contract is very narrow at a given point, this may be the time to buy a contract (establish a long position by agreeing to purchase), especially if recent tracking results indicate that the spread is likely to be much wider on the contract maturity date. Once established, a futures hedge can also be "unwound" by taking the opposite approach (establishing a short position, or agreeing to sell), thereby assuring the bank of a hedging effort that effectively protects its cash position.

Tracking basis spread is an ongoing process, preferably to be done as daily proposition. A computer program that handles this task and provides projections as to where the basis is likely to be at various points in the future can be most helpful. But basis tracking is only part of a truly functional futures program; the portfolio (investments) manager must also have the flexibility and authority to take fast action, whenever appropriate, to take advantage of anticipated basis point spreads.

Designing the Hedge Decision-Making Process

Each bank must design a hedge decision-making process that suits its own needs and satisfies the directives of its investment philosophy. The bank that is using futures contracts as a hedging mechanism may find it necessary or desirable to appoint one person as the *trader*, the person who has the authority to contact the broker and effect the sales and purchases of the contracts. This in-house trader is not to be confused with the individual on the floor of the exchange who actually places the orders when directed to do so by the bank through its broker. The bank's in-house trader probably will never see the floor of the exchange but will simply place telephone calls to the broker, who notifies the floor trader to effect sales and purchases of futures contracts as the bank sees fit.

The bank's trader may or may not have full authority to initiate futures transactions on their own. There may be a committee, or perhaps one or two key individuals, who must pass judgment on the trader's decisions before a futures contract order is actually placed. These other individuals may be the portfolio manager (if other than the trader), the ALCO chairperson, or someone in the bank's formal Investments or Financial Planning Department. Whatever process is established must be fast-acting and flexible, however, if full advantage is to be taken of opportunities in the futures market. While a double check on the trader's proposed moves in this market is always a good idea, the system must be such that this can be accomplished quickly and decisively.

The bank's decision-making process should help the trader determine when to buy or sell a futures contract. Regardless of how streamlined the bank's system may be, it should always include the following steps.

1. *Define the risk*. The trader must be able to determine, and demonstrate to the parties who must approve the plan, the amount of risk the bank assumes when it buys or sells a particular contract on the futures market.

2. *Select the futures contract or contracts*. Some contract types may be more favorable than others in a given situation. Both the bank's in-house trader and anyone who

must approve the proposed moves in the futures market need to be able to make this determination.
3. *Choose the contract month (when it must be satisfied) based on liquidity considerations and convergence.* Convergence is the point at which there is no longer a market value that might exceed the stated value of the contract. In general, basis points are sacrificed as time goes by. This is because there is a risk in time. As the contract expiration date approaches, less uncertainty exists.
4. *Determine the hedge ratio—a weighted dollar value of the contract.* This involves using duration analysis to establish the true value of the contract today in relation to the projected market upon contract maturity.

Each of these steps in the hedge decision-making process is presented in greater detail in the following discussions. They may seem complicated, at first, but as the bank gains experience in using the futures market as a hedging tool, most of these steps will be accomplished quickly and without delay. While the bank's in-house trader is generally charged with the responsibility of making decisions and taking these steps, advice is usually available from other bank experts, especially those who have approval authority over proposed futures market transactions.

Defining the Risk

To the extent possible, futures contract risks should be defined in terms of dollar amounts, rather than percentages. The risk, here, is the dollar amount of exposure to a given change in interest rates over a specific period of time. The risk is more easily defined with instruments involving LIBOR than with many other types of investments or hedging techniques, because the cost per basis point on each $1 million contract has been established at $25.

For example, if a bank borrows $1 million for 90 days at LIBOR, the exposure, or risk, on that contract is $25 for each basis point of upward movement in rate. If LIBOR is 6% and the market rate is projected to move up .8% by the contract maturity date, then the risk is 80 basis points. Multiplying this times the $25 cost per point gives a total risk of $2,000. Whether this exposure is acceptable is the bank's decision.

The market interest rate could move down during the 90-day term of the contract. If so, the bank's exposure decreases accordingly. Should the situation reach the point at which current rates are actually lower than LIBOR, the bank cannot take advantage of this fact, unless it can find a buyer for the contract and effect a swap or other deal that enables it to realize a greater return than is being provided by the LIBOR rate. This is not necessarily an impossible task, since there may be a buyer (speculator) who thinks the interest rate trend will reverse itself before the contract matures. But a decision to reverse the hedge must be made far enough in advance for that buyer to be found, because basis points are sacrificed as time passes (see the discussion below on liquidity and convergence).

Selecting the Appropriate Futures Contract

In many ways, selecting the appropriate futures contract—or deciding what underlying instrument(s) to use for a futures contract—is similar to the matching technique discussed earlier in this book. The objective is to hedge against potential loss due to unfavorable shifts in market interest rates by obtaining an offsetting instrument that is not to be paid for (or on which full payment will not be received) until a specified point in the future. When that date arrives, the contract must be honored by both buyer and seller, regardless of where rates lie at the moment. This is why accurate projection techniques are especially critical to hedging in the futures market.

While the exact instruments and contracts to use depend on the situation, including the bank's investment philosophy, some common combinations are:

- *Use a bond future to hedge against basis risk.* Bond rates are traditionally low in comparison to the rates obtainable on other types of instruments, but they are virtually guaranteed. Therefore, bonds make an excellent hedge against at least a portion of the earnings risk (including basis risk) a bank may be facing.

- *Use money market instruments to hedge against LIBOR risks.* If projections indicate that LIBOR on one or more transactions is likely to fall short of what could be earned, an offsetting investment in future money market funds can make up at least some of the difference. The higher money market instrument rates could more than offset the LIBOR exposure; or the exposure could be increased, rather than alleviated, if projections are incorrect. In general, however, this type of offsetting contract in the futures market could prove very helpful when the bank is locked in to a loss on LIBOR and anticipates an increase in market interest rates.

- *Use a LIBOR futures contract to offset potential exposure on commercial paper.* A guaranteed LIBOR rate, while not necessarily a real money-maker for the bank, could protect it against a potential business failure on the part of a large commercial loan customer. Clearly, the entire loss cannot be offset in this manner; but a portion of it can be transferred to a speculator or other investor who is in the market for commercial paper.

ASSET/LIABILITY MANAGEMENT TECHNIQUES

Any number of possible combinations of futures contracts can be used to protect against anticipated risks. Not all of these combinations are necessarily acceptable to bank management; some may seem too risky in themselves to receive approval. Further, bank regulations might come into play with certain types of futures contracts. These are all factors that must be made clear to in-house traders, since this knowledge will help them avoid presenting futures transactions that are simply unacceptable.

Selecting the Contract Month

Futures contracts are available in quarterly increments. The bank can elect to assume a long or a short position for a period of several quarterly increments, however, so a decision must be made as to the maturity date of the futures contract. Both liquidity and convergence (discussed shortly) must be considered in making this month-of-maturity decision.

Contracts on the futures market generally provide a great deal of liquidity. Up to the point at which the maturity date looms too near, these contracts can be bought, sold, or swapped for others that appear to present a more favorable situation for the bank. From the standpoint of liquidity, then, futures contracts are often beneficial.

A point is reached in any futures contract, however, beyond which there is little advantage to another party to buy it. The purchaser of an existing futures contract is usually anticipating a basis point advantage. He or she feels that the basis point spread will be sufficient upon contract maturity to allow them to make money. As the maturity date approaches, however, the existence (or lack) of a basis spread advantage becomes increasingly obvious. Ultimately, the point is reached at which either the bank can make a profit (or achieve the desired protection, at least), or it is clear that there will be a basis loss on the contract. In the first instance, it would be unwise for the bank to sell the contract. And in the second case, it is unlikely that a buyer can be found who is willing to accept the inevitable loss on the contract. This point is known as *convergence*, because it is where the cash price and the futures price of the contract converge. The basis spread advantage (or disadvantage) is too obviously established to make the contract worth buying or selling.

Up to a point that is fairly close to convergence, the bank can usually buy or sell a futures contract on the market. Speculators who are willing to take risks of this nature for the chance of relatively high gains are usually looking for the opportunity to buy a still-viable contract. If a bank holding such a contract faces an unexpected liquidity crisis, there may be an advantage to obtaining the ready cash that can be realized on the contract, even if some amount of loss is incurred in the transaction. Basis advantage is given up as time passes, however; and once the point of convergence is reached, it is too late to take action on that particular futures contract.

Careful tracking and projection of the basis curve (see Figure 6) help indicate the likely convergence point on a futures contract. This curve graphically demonstrates that point at which there is no longer any trade value in the contract. As the curve approaches zero, then perhaps even crosses the zero line, it is highly unlikely that a buyer can be found for the contract. The bank must then let the contract take its course and incur whatever profit or loss is provided by the then-prevailing basis position.

ASSET/LIABILITY MANAGEMENT TECHNIQUES

Determining the Hedge Ratio

As part of their standardization, futures contracts are available in $1 million units. Since the face amount of the item(s) to be hedged can total any amount, it becomes necessary to determine how many futures contracts of a particular type are needed to hedge the risk adequately. A hedge ratio is normally used for this purpose, with the hedger deciding that a certain number of a specific futures contract is needed to provide the desired risk protection.

Several factors must be considered when determining the hedge ratio. With interest rate hedges using futures contracts, the maturities of the contracts must approximate those of the items being hedged if protection is to be provided for a sufficient period. Further, the fair value (market value, not necessarily the same as the face value) of the item being hedged must be considered in determining the hedge ratio. Otherwise, the bank might obtain too few futures contracts to hedge the entire amount or, conversely, might obtain more contracts than it needs to hedge the true value of the hedged item(s).

A relatively simple hedge ratio that takes both the maturity and the volatility of the hedged item into consideration follows:

Hedge ratio = Maturity factor × Volatility factor

The maturity factor is based on the value of a basis point today, in cash, as opposed to the projected basis point value in the future. The volatility factor is based on the change in the current cash yield that can be obtained on the contract (or its underlying instruments), as compared to the change in the futures contract's yield. Note that *yields* are being used in this relationship, not cash or futures prices.

Substituting these stated factors into the hedge ratio formula presented above, the following explanation emerges:

$$\text{Hedge ratio} = \frac{\$\text{Value of bp (Cash)}}{\$\text{Value of bp (Futures)}} \times \frac{\text{Change in cash yield}}{\text{Change in futures yield}}$$

The hedge ratio is important because it helps the bank decide how many futures contracts it should use to hedge against the potential exposure presented by its portfolio in various projected interest rate scenarios. Selecting the appropriate projected rate, which has been discussed and emphasized repeatedly, is critical to the hedge ratio, because it impacts heavily on the factors involved in the hedge ratio formula.

The hedge ratio resulting from the above formula can be used at any time, since the bank's hedge decision-making procedures should provide it with those figures that cannot be readily obtained. For example, today's dollar value of a basis point can be determined from the current hedge market. So can the cash yield and current changes being experienced in it. The unknowns are the dollar value of each basis point at each future time frame, and the corresponding yield on the futures contract. These are the specific items that must be projected for use in the formula.

The hedge ratio relates the dollar movement of the value of a security to a given (assumed) interest rate. It indicates, through the mechanical calculation involved, what the future value of that security will be at each interest rate that is "plugged into" the formula. The future dollar value of each basis point can be calculated for each projected interest rate the bank's ALCO assumes to be logical. The resulting figure indicates the amount (and, therefore, the number) of futures contracts the bank must buy to protect its earnings position against the potential exposure presented by the transaction in question.

The accuracy of the hedge ratio can be double-checked using what is known as a *regression hedging* technique. In this process, past performances of various hedges—futures contracts, in particular—are plotted against what the ratio indicates should have happened with those contracts over the same period of time. If the results are essentially the same, then the formula is working; that is, the bank is accurately predicting interest rate movements and the resulting prices and yields on various types of investment instruments. If the figure derived from the hedge ratio formula is widely divergent from the actual performances of those instruments, then something (probably the projected interest rate) is inaccurate and must be recalculated or forecast by some means other than the one being used.

In futures contracts involving LIBOR, as noted, the value of each basis point is established at $25. With these contracts, the hedge ratio formula is unnecessary; the relationship between today's cash value per basis point and the predetermined $25 future value simplifies the determination of the cost of the hedge. But when the future value of a basis point must be determined, it can be projected by applying the hedge ratio formula to the known and projected values. This gives bank management an indication of the values it might anticipate on various futures contracts under different market interest rate scenarios.

Sample Hedge Ratio Application

The best way to demonstrate how to use the hedge ratio to determine how many futures contracts to buy in order

FUTURES AS A HEDGING TECHNIQUE

to solve a potential risk problem is to present an example. The following sample application of the hedge ratio technique and several of the other examples in this book were developed by Dr. Glenn C. Picou, Vice President, Citicorp Financial Futures Corporation. The sample problems are used here because they present outstanding examples of how exposure problems can be solved using the hedge ratio and various other techniques to determine the appropriate action to take in the futures market. Here are the parameters of the sample hedge ratio situation.

Scenario

On 1/6/84, the bank makes a $10 million, two-year fixed-rate loan that calls for quarterly interest payments with no amortization (no quarterly principal payback).

Initial funding is provided by six-month CDs at 10.32% (which is 3/16 over LIBOR) for 2/3/84-8/3/84.

The yield curve is normally sloped, and rates are expected to rise over the loan term.

Problem

How to hedge the CD rollover that will occur on 8/3/84.

While the amounts, rates, and dates would obviously vary from one situation to the next, the problem presented here is typical of what might be faced by a bank at any given time. The situation can be presented in graphic form, as illustrated in Figure 7. The area represented by the solid line (from 2/3/84 to 8/3/84) is hedged by the six-month CDs. The remaining time frames are not hedged, however, since the CDs mature and can be expected to roll over as of the 8/3/84 date. The unhedged time frames are indicated by a broken line in the schematic. The problem is to "fill the gap" by hedging the remaining time frames until the $10 million loan is repaid on 2/3/86.

Figure 7
Sample Hedge Ratio Problem Schematic

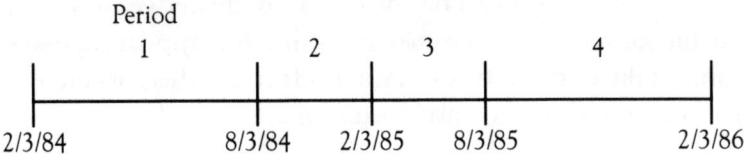

- The problem is to hedge the liability rate until the asset matures on 2/3/86.
- Period 1 is covered by the existing CD.

To complete the hedge of this loan, the bank must determine how many futures contracts to buy to cover its exposure. It should be noted that the entire period should be hedged. Later, the bank might borrow funds that would offset part of the remaining exposure on the loan it has made in the example. If so, it can buy back its futures contracts, or that portion of them that is no longer needed, perhaps saving money. A combination of the yield curve, the cash market, and the futures market indicates when it might be appropriate to buy back all or part of a futures contract. In this example, it is assumed that no such borrowing occurs, and the entire $10 million loan must be hedged between 8/3/84, when the CDs roll over, and 2/3/86, which is the date the loan is to be repaid.

The factors involved in using a hedge ratio to determine the action to take in the futures market are spelled out in Figure 8. Some of these factors are subjective, while others are strictly objective. For example, if the proposed futures contract involves a 90-day LIBOR, the known costs (as part of the standardization of futures contracts) are $25 per basis point. Further, the current cash value of each basis point can be established by market price, in this case, $50, and the future cash value should be $25. Simple division provides a maturity factor of 2. That is, based on these parameters, the volatility factor would be multiplied by 2 to determine how many futures contracts are needed per million dollars of the loan being hedged. These are all objectively established figures based on the standardized type of suggested futures contract involved.

At this point, however, subjective factors may come into play. For example, the A/L manager performs regressive hedging on six-month LIBOR against a Eurodollar futures contract and decides, based on his or her interpretation of market trends, that a maturity factor of less than 1 will be more accurate. The manager determines subjectively that a factor of .876 will suffice, and this is the figure he or she decides to multiply by the volatility factor (2). This reduces the number of futures contracts the manager feels the bank needs to hedge the exposed time frames of the loan.

Based on these considerations, the hedge ratio in this sample problem is determined by multiplying 2 times the anticipated volatility factor of .876. This indicates the need to sell 1.75 futures contracts per $1 million of the loan to be hedged, or a total of 17.5 contracts per time period involved in the overall hedge. Rounding this figure off in the event that no $500,000 contracts are available, the bank needs to sell 18 of the described futures contracts during each time period to hedge the entire $10 million loan.

In this situation, the bank is hedging three rollovers in six-month dollars. This can be changed, however, to three-month dollars, if desired, by buying back fewer futures con-

Figure 8
Using the Hedge Ratio Technique

- Volatility factor
  Regress six-month LIBOR vs. Eurodollar futures contract:
  Factor = .876 R^2 = .92

- Maturity factor
  $$\frac{\text{Basis point (Cash)}}{\text{Basis point (Futures)}} = \frac{\$50}{\$25} = 2$$

- Hedge ratio = 2×.876 = 1.75 contracts/$million, or to hedge $10 million, we need 17.5 contracts/time period.

tracts. In addition, while it may not be apparent, the bank has accomplished an 18-month hedge without getting locked into additional risk. The bank maintains flexibility by retaining the right to buy back whatever portion of these contracts it wishes, which enables it to adjust and manage its futures position as desired—within the confines of the convergence factor that were noted earlier.

The hedge ratio formula can be used to determine how many futures contracts are necessary to protect the bank against whatever exposure it incurs in buying and selling various assets and liabilities. It works well when relatively short-term instruments are involved (up to two or three years, for example) and when no amortization (principal payback) is involved. When the instruments or investments involved do not meet these criteria, however, other methods of deciding what action to take may come into play, such as the conversion factor hedge or the duration hedge technique. A brief discussion of each of these techniques follows.

Conversion Factor Hedge Technique

The bank may decide to use a technique known as the conversion factor hedge to protect against exposure on long-term bond purchases. In the United States, conversion factor hedges are transacted with other futures contracts on the same exchange, the Chicago Mercantile Exchange. The objectives of conversion factor hedges on bonds are to provide protection against risk exposure while still realizing at least some profit on the bond.

The CME has established certain criteria which a bond must meet before it can be delivered into a futures contract on the exchange. First, the bond must be 15 years to call (its maturity must be at least 15 years), and the transaction involving such a bond is based on an eight percent standard rate. In other words, if the bank takes a bond at eight percent, this is the same rate it will pay for a futures contract to hedge that instrument. When this is the case, a dollar-for-dollar exchange exists, and the hedge accomplishes only one of its objectives: It provides the desired hedge against risk. Therefore, it is worthwhile from that standpoint, although this stance precludes making a profit on the transaction.

If a profit is to be realized on the bond itself, something other than a dollar-for-dollar exchange must be effected. This is where the conversion factor is implemented, since it is a device that will enable the hedger to realize a profit on the bond, as well as protect against exposure. With this approach, the conversion factor *is* the hedge ratio. It is actually an adjustment factor that compensates for coupon differences on delivery (when the bond matures). The higher the coupon difference on any bond, the higher the conversion factor must be. And a higher conversion factor will result in an indication that more offsetting futures contracts are required both to offset the risk and to generate earnings on the transaction.

Multiplying the conversion factor times the futures price tells the bank what it should be willing to pay for any given bond. Thus, if the conversion factor (which equals the hedge ratio) works out at 1.5, then the bank is short 1.5 futures and must obtain them to hedge the bond successfully. Figure 9, from Dr. Picou, demonstrates the elements involved and their relationships. Two bond types are illustrated: cheapest to deliver, and any other bond.

In each case, the maturity factor approximately equals the conversion factor. The conversion factor for the cheapest-to-deliver bond is calculated by dividing the cheapest value of a basis point (VBP) today by the anticipated futures value of a basis point. The resulting figure indicates the number of futures contracts required to hedge the bond. If this division results in a conversion factor of 1.5, for example, then the bank is short 1.5 futures; this is the number of futures contracts required, in other words, to hedge the bond.

Figure 9
Conversion Factor Hedges

For cheapest to deliver bond:
$$\text{Maturity factor} = \text{Conversion factor} = \frac{\text{VBP (cheapest)}}{\text{VBP (Futures)}}$$

For any other bond:
$$\text{Maturity factor} = \text{Conversion factor} \times \frac{\text{VBP (Bond)}}{\text{VBP (cheapest)}}$$

For any bond other than cheapest-to-deliver, the conversion factor, which approximately equals the maturity factor, must be multiplied by the result obtained when the value of a basis point on the bond is divided by the value of a basis point on the cheapest-to-deliver bond. As before, the resulting figure indicates how many futures contracts the bank needs to hedge the bond in question.

While the conversion factor hedge ratio obtained for either of these bond types (cheapest or other) is generally accurate, consideration must be made as to any special activity the particular bond consistently demonstrates. For example, if the conversion factor is 1.5 for the cheapest-to-deliver bond, but the bond being hedged moves 20% more than that cheapest bond, an adjustment must be made to compensate for this fact. The bank must use 20% more futures than indicated by the conversion factor ratio or the bond will not be properly hedged. Careful tracking of historic bond movements is in order for banks that are active in the bond market and who want to hedge those instruments in the futures market.

In summary, with the cheapest-to-deliver bond, the conversion factor directly reflects the number of futures contracts required for an effective hedge. For any other bond, that is, any bond whose movements are greater than the cheapest—the conversion factor must be multiplied by the ratio of the basis point values of the cheapest-to-deliver bond and the one in question.

Figure 10 provides an example of the potential earnings on the cash market compared to those that might be obtained on a long conversion-factor-weighted hedge in the futures market.

In this comparison, the portfolio manager wants to buy bonds at a specified time based on anticipated cash flows into the bank. This can be accomplished either on a cash basis, which means waiting until the anticipated cash flow

ASSET/LIABILITY MANAGEMENT TECHNIQUES

becomes a reality, or by moving now to buy the bonds in the futures market. If the manager prefers to buy on the cash market, he or she must wait until they have the $1 million—the anticipated cash flow—to invest in the 10-3/8% bonds. The current price is 86.20, so the million-dollar investment on the cash market would cost $860,625.00, if the manager could buy the bonds today.

On the other hand, the portfolio manager could decide to go ahead and buy the same bonds by taking advantage of the futures market. The conversion factor on the 10-3/8% rate is 1.2499, which rounds off at 1.25. The manager wants to hedge the cheapest-to-deliver bond in $100,000 futures contract increments, so he or she decides to buy 13 treasury bond futures at 68.30—a cost of $68,937.50 per contract, or a total of $896,187.50.

The comparison of these two approaches can only be appreciated by observing what happens when the portfolio manager decides to unwind the hedge bought in the futures market. If the anticipated cash flow has occurred, those same bonds could be purchased now at the same rate of 10-3/8%. But at this point, the price is $100.18, so to buy the same bonds will cost the bank a total of $1,005,625. The net result is that the portfolio manager, by waiting until the cash flows materialized instead of purchasing the bonds in the futures market when originally considering them, has cost the bank $145,000, an unnecessary opportunity loss.

Conversely, the manager who took advantage of the futures market can sell those bonds at this same point in time. Since the price is now $100.18, the bank realizes a hedge position gain of $11,156.25 per contract. With 13 contracts to sell, the bank nets $145,031.25 instead of losing approximately that amount with a decision to wait until the anticipated cash flows became a reality.

Figure 10
Comparison of Cash and Futures Market Hedges

Long Hedge—Conversion Factor Weighted

	Cash Market	Futures Market
Initiate hedge	Portfolio manager decides to invest $1 million projected cash flow in 10⅜'s Current price = 86.20 ($860,625.00)	Buy 13 T-bond futures @68.30 ($68,937.50)
Unwind hedge	Purchase 10⅜'s Current price = 100.18 ($1,005,625)	Sell 13 T-bond futures @80.03 ($80,093.75)
Result	Opportunity loss (higher price) of $145,000	Hedge position gain of: $11,156.25 per contract x13 contracts $145,031.25

The conversion factor hedge is helpful in determining how many futures contracts are needed to hedge a long-term instrument, such as a bond. This technique enables the portfolio manager to take advantage of bond opportunities as they arise, while still effectively hedging the bank's position against earnings exposure. Conversion may seem complicated at first, but experience in using this tool helps portfolio managers gain confidence in their ability to provide the bank with the protection it needs for long-term investments. Whenever a bond has 15 or more years to call, it can be delivered into a futures contract in the manner described here. With the protection that can be attained through the futures market, the bank has greater flexibility in deciding when and how much to invest in long-term bonds, thereby broadening its potential earnings capability.

ASSET/LIABILITY MANAGEMENT TECHNIQUES

The Duration Hedge Technique

The duration hedge technique is especially applicable to long-term instruments, such as mortgage loans, on which amortization occurs—periodic payments reduce the principal balance over time. These cash flows must be taken into consideration if the true amount of exposure is to be established for hedging purposes.

Duration is a measurement of price responsiveness to a change in yield. Securities which have equal durations also have equivalent price sensitivity to interest rates, assuming parallel yield curve shifts occur. If the yield curves shift in such a way that they are no longer parallel, an adjustment must be made to keep the hedge in balance. If a particular security has a duration of 5, then it presents the same exposure to risk as any other security with a duration of 5 over the same period of time. This is true as long as the yield curves parallel each other, as noted. In addition, this concept can be extended to include an entire portfolio, not just two individual securities, so the duration technique can be used to provide effective hedges that protect the bank's exposure across its entire portfolio.

Calculating Duration

A duration hedge is equivalent to an "01" hedge, which is the terminology used to indicate that it provides a one-to-one offset in the futures market to securities obtained or held today. This is possible because duration takes into consideration all dollar flows on the instrument, not just those that are scheduled to occur at maturity. Duration represents an attempt to adjust the bank's cash position to match its futures position, or vice-versa, thereby minimizing, if not completely offsetting, earnings exposure.

FUTURES AS A HEDGING TECHNIQUE

The formula for calculating the duration hedge ratio (DHR) is:

$$\text{DHR} = \frac{\text{Percentage change in price}}{\text{Change in interest rate}}$$

The result of this calculation is the hedge ratio, which indicates the number of futures contracts needed to hedge against the anticipated exposure. An accurate hedge ratio cannot be obtained simply by comparing the ratios of two durations. Instead, the anticipated percentage change in a security's price must be divided by the change in interest rate on that security, which provides the desired "01" hedge value of that security upon maturity.

This 01 duration hedge figure can then be used to determine the 01 value for cash, which is the bank's current position. That is, the duration figure resulting from the formula, when applied to today's cost of a security, indicates the true value of that security at the moment based on current price, rates, and maturity factors. This is a "weighted" value that takes cash flows into consideration. Comparing this figure to the 01 value for futures indicates the number of futures contracts needed to effect the hedge.

Duration is not a one-time calculation, since it is based on projections that may or may not be totally accurate. It must be tracked and recalculated regularly (daily, if the bank has the capability to do so), and adjustments must be made to compensate for price and rate shifts. If the calculation indicates, for example, that more or fewer futures contracts are needed to hedge the risk as price and rate factors change, the portfolio manager can take the necessary action to maintain the appropriate hedge of the bank's position.

Because both the cash and futures positions are calculated for an 01 hedge through application of the formula, the resulting figures for both represent weighted values. They are weighted in the sense that they provide relative values assuming that the investments being compared are subjected to the same price, rate, and cash flow fluctuations. As a result, duration analysis provides a highly accurate assessment of the anticipated gap between assets and liabilities in the portfolio (see Figure 11).

Figure 11
Duration—Hedging the Gap

Assets	Liabilities
$D(A) =$ Weighted sum of asset duration	$D(L) =$ Weighted sum of liability duration

$$D(GAP) = D(A) - D(L)$$

This technique works for both assets and liabilities in the portfolio. The difference between asset duration and liability duration, when determined for the entire portfolio, indicates the bank's overall position in light of the entire portfolio. Once this is established, the portfolio manager can take steps in the futures market to protect the bank against that exposure.

The difference between the weighted sum of asset duration and the weighted sum of liability duration is, in fact, the gap that must be hedged. The *weighting* factor in this instance pertains to the weighted prices of the instruments. The entire portfolio is represented in this calculation, although the comparison and resulting gap can be obtained on individual instruments (assets and liabilities) in the same manner. This analysis can also be applied to the entire balance sheet, in addition to the investment portfolio, which

FUTURES AS A HEDGING TECHNIQUE

can be used to determine if additional adjustments should be made.

Duration analysis is just one of several techniques that can be used to determine whether a gap exists that must be hedged in some manner. It is most helpful when long-term assets and liabilities are involved, since it takes into consideration the cash flows that frequently occur with several types of long-term instruments. As with the other techniques discussed in this book, duration is only as accurate as the bank's ability to anticipate interest rate and price shifts. When these projections are on target, duration analysis presents an extremely accurate estimate of the gap that must be hedged. This provides the portfolio manager with meaningful direction as to the actions to take in the futures market to protect and enhance the bank's position.

Summary

Buying and selling contracts in the futures market represents a viable means of hedging a bank's position against exposure. Futures contracts are easy to use because they are standardized and are all traded, domestically, through one exchange—the Chicago Board of Trade. Contract costs are relatively low, and they can be bought or sold at will as long as there still is sufficient value in them to make such a transaction worthwhile to both parties.

With futures, only the initial margin deposit is required up-front. The broker makes additional margin calls when the account falls below the maintenance margin; or the hedger can withdraw the amounts by which the account exceeds the maintenance margin. The low initial cash outlay helps preserve the bank's capital (cash) position. This factor, combined with the flexibility that exists in the contracts themselves (ability to buy or sell as desired), helps the bank maintain an advantageous liquidity position. By far the greatest advantage of a futures contract, however, is the opportunity it presents to shift risk from the bank to another party, often a speculator who feels certain that market interest rates will move in a favorable direction.

Because there is an established exchange, the portfolio manager can also use the futures market as a price discovery mechanism. A call to the broker with whom the bank deals can tell the manager a great deal about where the experts working on the exchange think interest rates are likely to be at various points in the future. The exchange clearly states what LIBOR rates are applicable on different instruments, another clear indication of anticipated interest rate movements.

The interest yield curve drives basis, which is the cash price minus the futures price. Basis risk, in fact, is a primary determinant as to whether a bank should pay cash for a given instrument or buy it on the margin in the futures market. A logical approach to this market—one that involves defining the risk, selecting the appropriate futures contract and maturity month, and determining the hedge ratio to establish how many futures contracts to buy or sell—enables the portfolio manager to obtain the risk protection the bank needs and perhaps generate additional earnings in the process.

The hedge ratio, which involves multiplying the maturity factor of an instrument by its volatility factor, is not the only means of determining how many futures contracts are needed. The manager can use a conversion factor hedge for long-term (15 years or more) bonds; and the duration hedging technique can be used for even longer-term instruments, such as mortgages, especially those whose principal is amortized over their terms. The best technique depends on the type of instrument being hedged. Regardless of instrument type, however, an effective hedge can usually be accomplished by buying or selling futures contracts that offset the risk to which the bank is exposed.

Futures represent just one of many tools available for investment portfolio management and earnings risk protection. They can be important to a bank that has a widely varying portfolio and should certainly be considered as hedges against potential losses on both the asset and liability sides of the balance sheet. With the approval of management, the portfolio manager can use futures extensively to obtain effective hedges against losses to which the bank is exposed through its investment activities.

4
Options as Hedges

An option is a contract in which one party (the buyer) obtains the right, but not the obligation, to buy or sell an item from or to a second party (the writer of the option) at a specified price and at a stated time. The contract term is called the *exercise period*, since the buyer can exercise the right to buy or sell at any point during this time. Every option contract is either a *put* or a *call* option. The buyer of a call option pays a premium (fee) for the right to buy the specified item or items at a stipulated price, known as the *strike* price. And the buyer of a put option pays a premium for the right to sell an item to the other party at a stated strike price.

Meanwhile, the writer (seller) of a put option agrees to accept delivery of the stipulated item at the strike price. And the writer of a call option agrees to deliver the item stated in the contract at the stipulated price. In exchange, the writer receives the option premium, usually immediately, minus the margin deposit that is required by the broker handling the transaction. The elements of an option contract are shown in Figure 12.

The exercise period of the contract, the specific item(s) involved, the price at which the writer will sell (deliver) or buy (take delivery of) the item, and the amount paid by the option buyer to obtain the right to buy or sell (the option premium) are all established at the time the contract is initiated. The unknown factor in an option situation is the market price fluctuations the underlying item might undergo during the exercise term. This is the determining factor in whether the buyer will exercise the option at any given time. How accurately the parties project these market price fluc-

ASSET/LIABILITY MANAGEMENT TECHNIQUES

**Figure 12
Elements of an Option**

```
                                    OPTION
                                                      AT EXPIRATION
                                                      OR EARLIER
      AT INCEPTION         DURING THE TERM            EXERCISE

    ┌──────────────┐    IF PRICES MOVE IN FAVOR    IF OPTION HAS
    │  COMPANY A   │       OF THE WRITER...        VALUE ("IN THE
    │   (BUYER)    │                                  MONEY")
    └──────────────┘    ┌──────────────────────┐
           │            │ USUALLY NO CASH      │   ┌──────────────┐
           │            │ CHANGES HANDS—MARGIN │   │  COMPANY A   │
        $  │  OPTION    │ USUALLY IS NOT       │   │   (BUYER)    │
           │  PREMIUM   │ REFUNDABLE UNTIL     │   └──────────────┘
           │            │ THE OPTION IS        │          ↑
           ▼            │ EXERCISED OR EXPIRES │       $  │  SETTLEMENT*
    ┌──────────────┐    └──────────────────────┘   ┌──────────────┐
    │    BROKER    │                                │    BROKER    │
    └──────────────┘                                └──────────────┘
           ▲            IF PRICES MOVE IN FAVOR    IF OPTION EXPIRES
           │               OF THE BUYER...         WORTHLESS ("OUT
                                                   OF THE MONEY")
  OPTION         MARGIN  ⎫                          
  PREMIUM  $ $   DEPOSIT ⎬ PAID  ┌──────────────┐   ┌──────────────┐
                         ⎭ NET   │    BROKER    │   │    BROKER    │
           │                     └──────────────┘   └──────────────┘
           │                            ↑                  │
           │                         $  │ ADDITIONAL    $  │ RETURN
           │                            │ MARGIN           │ MARGIN
           ▼                            │ DEPOSITS         ▼ DEPOSITS
    ┌──────────────┐                ┌──────────────┐   ┌──────────────┐
    │  COMPANY B   │                │  COMPANY B   │   │  COMPANY B   │
    │  (WRITER)    │                │  (WRITER)    │   │  (WRITER)    │
    └──────────────┘                └──────────────┘   └──────────────┘

   *ASSUMING CASH SETTLEMENT IN LIEU OF DELIVERY.
```

Reprinted with permission of Price Waterhouse from *Hedging: Foreign Exchange and Interest Rate Risk Management Implementation Guide.* Copyright © 1986 Price Waterhouse. All rights reserved.

tuations determines whether they will gain, lose, or break even on the option contract.

Roles of the Parties to an Option

Unlike most other contracts, an option is one-sided in that the buyer can exercise it at any time during its term or can simply let it expire without exercising the right to buy or sell at the stipulated price. The writer, on the other hand, has no recourse if the buyer decides to exercise the option. The writer must deliver or accept delivery of the specified item at the strike price any time the buyer decides to exercise the option prior to contract expiration. Further, the writer has no means of forcing the buyer to exercise the option. If the buyer elects not to do so, there is nothing the writer can do about it. The buyer is in control of the situation from inception to expiration (or prior exercise) of the option.

At first glance, it might seem unwise for anyone to be the writer of an option contract. There is an immediate advantage, however, in that the writer receives the option premium in cash when the contract is initiated. This option premium is usually received through a broker whose role includes that of intermediary between writer and buyer. The writer actually receives the net between the option premium and the required margin deposit. A party needing quick cash might find it advantageous to assume the role of the writer of an option contract in exchange for the premium paid by the buyer.

The writer might be a speculator who anticipates that the price of the underlying item will remain favorable to him or her for the entire exercise period, thereby precluding the likelihood that the buyer will exercise the option. If this occurs, the writer receives the full amount of the option premium, including the margin deposit, which is returned upon expiration of the option. The writer (in this instance, a speculator) earns a profit in the form of the option premium and earnings on that money over the exercise period without ever having delivered anything to the buyer.

ASSET/LIABILITY MANAGEMENT TECHNIQUES

During the term of the contract, if the market price of the item(s) covered by an unexercised option moves in favor of the buyer, the writer will be required to make additional margin deposits. These deposits effectively reduce the amount of the premium the writer received upon option inception. If the price moves in favor of the writer, however, the writer does not usually receive a return of the margin deposits unless that favorable position persists when the contract expires. Technically, the writer would receive a return of all the margin deposits—in effect, receiving the total amount of the option premium—if the option were exercised while prices were favorable to him or her. However, it is unlikely that the buyer would exercise the option with the price favorable to the writer.

As this discussion indicates, it is not impossible for the option writer to make money on such a contract. If the writer correctly anticipates the price movement of the underlying financial instrument(s), he or she will ultimately receive the full amount of the premium, since the margin deposits will be returned upon contract expiration. In the meantime, the writer has the use of the net premium (full premium minus initial margin requirement) deposited with the broker by the buyer. Therefore, there is motivation for the option writer, despite the fact that the decision to exercise the option or let it expire lies entirely with the buyer.

The risks to the option writer must be fully understood. First, the writer's (seller's) profit is limited to the full amount of the premium they received. Further, the risks are high (they can, in fact, be unlimited) because the buyer can exercise the option at any time. This means that the writer could be required to deliver, on demand, some very costly financial instruments to the buyer. Because the risks are so high, banks using options to hedge interest rate risks usually do not serve the role of option writers. But under the proper circumstances, a bank might do well to be the buyer in an option contract.

As the option buyer, the bank can use the contract as an effective hedge, depending on its current and anticipated positions. For example, buyers may find it worthwhile to pay the required premium to assure the availability of certain financial instruments they may need within the exercise period. The buyer's risk never exceeds the potential loss of the premium paid for the option, since the strike price of the underlying instruments, and therefore the contract, is established at its inception. Loss of the premium is a small risk in comparison to the potentially unlimited exposure that might be incurred by the option writer should they be forced to deliver the stipulated financial instruments at a very unfavorable cost.

Exchange-Traded and Custom Options

The terms of exchange-traded options have been standardized for various underlying financial instruments to simplify trading and to provide stability to the market. The prices, exercise periods, and margin requirements are stipulated in these standardized contracts. This makes exchange-traded options especially liquid, since they can be bought and sold on a same-day basis should such activity be advantageous to the bank.

On the other hand, the standardized characteristics of exchange-traded options may be too restrictive to enable the bank to attain its asset/liability management objectives. Therefore, much of the effective option trading done for A/L management purposes is accomplished with customized contracts on an over-the-counter basis. The buyer or writer, usually through a broker, indicates the terms of the desired option. The broker then locates, via the over-the-counter market, another party who is willing to accept the deal. Thus, an option contract can be transacted efficiently and quickly, making it a potentially useful tool for the knowledgeable asset/liability manager.

Determining Option Status

The status of an option contract at any given time is determined by establishing the relationship between the strike price and the spot (current cash market) price of the underlying financial instruments. An option may be *in the money*, *out of the money*, or *at the money*, depending on this relationship. The status also depends on whether the contract constitutes a call option or a put option.

With a call option, the option buyer has the right to buy the underlying instruments at the strike price. If the strike price is lower than the spot price, the call option is said to be in the money. The holder (buyer) of this in the money call option can exercise the right to buy (call) at the strike price, then immediately sell the instruments in the spot market, thereby realizing a profit on the option.

A put option (one in which the option buyer has the right to put, or sell, at the strike price) is in the money when the strike price of the underlying instruments is greater than the spot market price. In this situation, the option holder can realize a profit by buying the specified instruments in the spot market, then selling them to the option writer at the strike price. The writer must accept the instruments at the strike price when the buyer exercises this put option, even though those same instruments are available at a lower price in the spot market.

An option contract is said to be out of the money when the opposite situations (to those described above) exist. That is, a call option is out of the money when the strike price is higher than the spot price. There would be no advantage to the option holder (buyer) to exercise a call option in this instance, since he or she can buy the same instruments at a lower price in the spot market. Conversely, with a put option, a strike price that is lower than the spot price makes this an out of the money situation. The buyer would be better off selling the instruments in the spot market instead of exercising the option and requiring the seller to buy them at the lower-than-spot price. Clearly, the factors determining whether an option is in or out of the money include the type of option involved (put or call) and the relationship between the strike and spot prices of the underlying instrument(s).

An at the money option, whether a put or a call, is one that represents a break-even for both parties. If the advantage that the buyer can gain by exercising a put or call approximately equals the amount of the option premium, there is no real advantage to exercising the option. As noted, the buyer is in control of the situation and can exercise the option at any time during the period stipulated in the contract. Unless a point is reached at which a real advantage can be gained, the buyer can simply let the option's exercise period (the contract term) expire without taking any action.

Most of the time, option settlements are made in cash. When buyers exercise their option to buy or sell, they are usually less interested in the underlying financial instruments than in the financial gain to be made by buying or selling at that time. There are exceptions, such as when the buyer needs a specific type of financial instrument to make delivery on some other contractual commitment. In most cases, however, the writer neither delivers nor accepts the actual underlying instruments. Instead, cash settlement is made if the buyer decides to exercise the option.

Elements of the Option Premium

The option premium paid by the buyer at contract inception has two elements: the intrinsic (inherent) value, and the time value. The intrinsic value is the degree to which the option is in the money. Therefore, an out-of-the-money or an at-the-money option has no intrinsic value. An option's time value equals the total premium minus the intrinsic value. Since out-of-the money and at-the-money options have no intrinsic values, the time values of such option contracts represent the total premium paid by the buyer.

The time value element of the premium compensates the writer for accepting the risk that the option will be in the money at some point before the exercise period expires. And if the option already has an intrinsic value at inception, the time value compensates the writer for the risk that it will be even further in the money during the contract term.

In determining the option premium to be paid by the buyer, several factors influence the time value. For example, if the prices of the underlying items are volatile, the chances are greater that the buyer might be in a position to exercise the option at some time during the exercise period. Therefore, the option premiums for contracts on these items are higher. The same is true with options that have longer exercise periods. The seller requires a higher premium payment because the longer contract term increases the possibility of having to accept or deliver the underlying financial instruments at a disadvantageous price.

The time value element of the option premium is also affected by whether the option is at the money, or close to at the money, when it is initiated. Again, with an option in this condition, chances are often greater that the buyer will exercise it at a time that puts the seller at a disadvantage. Therefore, the seller is justified in requiring a higher premium as protection against this increased risk.

Current short-term interest rates can also have an effect on the amount of the option premium. This effect depends on whether a put or a call option is involved. With a call option, increases in short-term interest rates generally increase the time value element of the option premium. Conversely, short-term interest rate increases tend to decrease the time value element of the premium required on puts. These effects are due to the inverse relationship between interest rates and prices of financial instruments (as interest rates increase, prices decrease, and vice-versa). Therefore, the premium required by the seller will vary with interest rate movements at contract inception and the nature (call or put) of the option.

At any time during the term of the contract, the intrinsic value can be determined, since it is the extent to which the option is in the money. For a call option, the intrinsic value is the amount by which the spot price exceeds the strike price. And for a put option, intrinsic value equals the amount by which the strike price exceeds the spot price. Once this determination is made, the remaining time value can also be calculated easily, since it is the difference between the option's current market price and its intrinsic value.

Using Options as Hedges

Options are often used as hedges against adverse movements in foreign currency costs. If a bank, company, or other entity will need a sum of a specific foreign currency at a certain time in the future, it can simply obtain those funds today on the spot market. This hedges the bank's position in the event that the dollar declines against the foreign currency in question. A simple forward contract can accomplish this same hedge without the immediate expenditure of the full amount.

There are some inherent risks to either of these actions, however. For instance, if the value of the foreign currency declines, the buyer loses rather than gains by having made its purchase or (with a forward) agreeing to buy at the higher price. Further, if the anticipated need for the foreign funds never materializes, the bank has created an uncovered exposure in the foreign currency.

As a logical alternative, the bank (or other entity) could decide to purchase an option on the foreign funds, exercising it when and if the money is actually needed. If the value of those funds then rises in relation to the dollar, the bank has "locked in" an advantage in the lower strike price. And if the foreign currency has moved in the opposite direction by the time it is needed, making it more advantageous for the bank to buy the necessary funds in the spot market than to exercise the option, all the buyer has lost is the premium. Clearly, an option to buy a specified amount of foreign currency to satisfy an anticipated need can provide an important measure of protection against adverse fluctuations in the cost of those funds.

Options used to hedge interest rate risks can be more complicated than straightforward currency exchange hedges. Written options (in which the hedger serves as the writer) are difficult to use as hedges. While they are construed by some to provide a measure of price protection (to the extent of the option premium received) in at-the-money situations, written hedges must generally begin and stay well in the money to serve a viable hedging function. The extremely high potential risks of written options make

OPTIONS AS HEDGES

them difficult to justify as hedges for most banks in their asset/liability management efforts.

Options in which the bank acts as the buyer can be used to provide the advantages discussed earlier. A bank can hedge interest rate risks without increasing exposure beyond the amount of the premium that must be paid to the option seller (writer). If the market for the underlying financial instruments moves favorably for the option buyer, an outright profit can be made by exercising the right to buy or sell. Options are generally easy to buy and, if desired, sell, providing liquidity that might not be available with other hedging tools. In many respects, then, options can and do serve as effective hedging tools for the knowledgeable A/L manager.

Several factors must be taken into consideration in selecting the option to be purchased, including:

- *The appropriate hedge ratio.* A one-on-one match-up between the amount to be hedged and the options available is not always possible. The buyer must determine as closely as possible how many option contracts (or the total option amount) are needed to provide an effective hedge.

- *The amount of premium required by the buyer.* This amount must be reasonable, or the purpose of the hedge might be defeated. One advantage to an option as a hedging tool is that the full value of the contract need not be paid upon purchase; only the premium is required. The A/L manager must make certain that the amount of the premium is in line with the hedge being effected.

- *Behavior of the option value in relation to the market value of the underlying instrument(s).* The price of option contracts that are deep in the money and at the money (strike price and spot price are approximately the same) closely follow the spot market prices of the underlying instruments. The change in dollar value of an option contract that is far out of the money, on the other hand, is usually significantly less than the change in value of the underlying item(s). Option contracts can be sold in the spot market, which makes it possible to maintain a measure of liquidity. The value of an option contract varies from the value of the underlying instruments in the spot market depending on the types of instruments involved and the nature of the market at the moment.

The asset/liability manager who is trying to maintain an options hedge at the same level throughout the term of the hedge is establishing a delta-neutral hedge. To accomplish this, the number of hedges will have to be increased or decreased during the exercise period to stay abreast of the changing values of the underlying instruments and, therefore, the option contracts used for the hedge. Careful monitoring of the values of option hedge contracts is necessary if the delta-neutral (no change) is to be maintained. The hedger can then buy or sell option contracts to keep the balance between the number of option contracts and the required hedge intact.

The use of options as hedges is growing in popularity, but the market is still adolescent compared to futures, swaps, and forwards in general. Options require close monitoring if they are to be used successfully. The A/L manager who is using options to hedge potential interest rate risks might have to make adjustments (buy or sell contracts) in the bank's position more frequently than with other techniques, especially when attempting to maintain a delta-neutral (no change) position. This is viewed as a disadvantage by many portfolio managers. Further, options generally cost more than futures and swaps due to the premium deposit that must be made at contract inception. Nevertheless, many banks have found option contracts to be extremely useful as hedges against interest rate risk exposure, especially since the option buyer stands to lose no more than the amount of the premium, regardless of fluctuations in market prices.

Accounting for Options

Generally accepted accounting practices for option contracts used as hedges are still being developed as of this writing. As with futures and swaps, options used as hedges are not accounted for in the same manner as other assets and liabilities. Instead, the guidelines found in FASB Statement 12 apply. Additional statements are contained in the 1986 AICPA Issues Paper, "Accounting for Options." The bank using options as a hedging technique must remain alert to the interpretations of these documents (Statement 12 and the Issues Paper) as they develop and are released as generally acceptable accounting practices.

In general, notations indicating the use of options must be entered at the time contracts for hedging purposes are initiated. As of this writing, the gains or losses incurred on option contracts are deferred until the option is exercised or the exercise period expires. This can vary according to the types of instruments underlying the option contract, however; and the accounting department of any bank using options as a hedging tool must stay abreast of official accounting guidelines for various types of options as those guidelines are released.

Summary

An option contract is one of the few truly one-sided contracts to be found in the financial arena. The contract writer agrees to deliver or accept delivery of the underlying financial instruments at any time the buyer so demands during the life (exercise period) of the contract. The buyer, on the other hand, is not required to deliver or accept the instruments. Therefore, the buyer will only exercise the option if the situation is to his or her advantage; the seller has no right to "force the issue" at any time.

Clearly, the writer of an option is at a disadvantage unless he or she receives compensation for the potentially unlimited risks involved. This compensation is provided in the form of the option premium paid by the buyer at contract inception. The seller is required to make an initial margin deposit with the broker, which reduces the amount of premium actually received at contract inception. Further, depending on price fluctuations during the life of the contract, the seller may have to make additional margin deposits, again reducing the amount of the premium actually retained. And if the option is exercised, it will virtually always be when there is an advantage to the buyer. In all these respects, the option contract seller is at a severe disadvantage and could incur significant losses.

Speculators are willing to write option contracts for two reasons. First, they can use the net premium received at contract inception for additional investments. And second, these speculators anticipate that the contract will be at the money or out of the money (or at least not sufficiently in the money to result in the buyer's exercising the option) throughout the exercise period. When this occurs and the contract expires, the seller's margin deposits are returned and the seller realizes the entire premium payment for the contract. Written options are seldom used as hedges by bank portfolio managers, but purchased option contracts can serve this pur-

OPTIONS AS HEDGES

pose, especially since the cost of the contract never exceeds the premium established and paid at inception.

Various aspects of exchange-traded option contracts have been standardized for use with a number of underlying financial instruments. Since these standardized contracts do not satisfy the needs of most hedgers, customized contracts are used more frequently for interest rate risk hedging purposes. In both cases, brokers serve as intermediaries between the parties to the contract. And, as with most such contracts, these parties probably will never meet; the entire transaction is handled through brokers (plus an exchange, if appropriate), with no direct contact between the parties themselves.

Even when the buyer exercises the option and calls for delivery (or decides to make delivery to the seller) of the financial instruments underlying an option contract, the actual instruments seldom change hands. Instead, cash settlements are made. The buyer usually exercises the option to buy or sell based on the difference between the strike price and the spot market price of the instruments. With the cash settlement from the option contract seller, the buyers can retain the profits made from the transaction, or buy whatever instruments are needed on the spot market at the favorable price that prompts them to exercise their option.

Because option contracts cost the buyer only the initial premium amount, and because these contracts can usually be sold at almost any time, they provide liquidity to the buyer. At the same time, the seller (contract writer) of the option receives the initial premium, minus the required margin deposit, upon contract inception, again providing liquidity in the form of cash. There are obvious advantages, then, to both the buyer and the writer of an option contract. Due to the high potential risks, however, written option contracts are seldom used by banks in their asset/liability management efforts. Banks usually serve as buyers in option contracts into which they enter.

Options can provide the asset/liability manager with an additional tool for use in protecting the bank's position against interest rate risk exposure. The potential exists to make a profit on option contracts, and this can be an additional benefit to using them as hedges against risk. But the hedging function these contracts can serve is probably the most important reason why a bank would enter into an option agreement.

5
Effective Portfolio Management

Effective portfolio management can be accomplished in many ways using a variety of tools and techniques, including those discussed thus far. The term *effective* has a wide range of meanings, however, since it is based entirely on what the bank expects its portfolio to do. A number of goals can be attained through portfolio management. Those attained by the portfolio manager must coincide with the bank's overall management plan and philosophy.

An investment portfolio is best thought of as just one element of the bank's total approach to financial management. The portfolio manager is an important member of the bank's management team, but is by no means *all* of it. Senior management must keep the portfolio manager fully informed as to its short- and long-term investment goals, providing general guidelines within which that person can adjust the portfolio daily, if necessary, to help attain those goals.

The portfolio manager (or someone from the same department) must be included on the ALCO. This enables him or her to see first-hand the bank's analysis of anticipated interest rate fluctuations, market trends, and various ideas that may or may not be adopted. Most important, the portfolio manager is exposed to senior management's thoughts concerning what is expected. With this knowledge in mind, the portfolio manager can do a much more effective job of manipulating the bank's assets and liabilities to satisfy its immediate and long-range needs.

ASSET/LIABILITY MANAGEMENT TECHNIQUES

Why the Portfolio Is Important

An investment portfolio plays at least two roles in most banks:

1. *An income role*, since significant income can be realized through proper management of the investments in the portfolio.
2. *A funding role*, because instruments (and groups of instruments) within the portfolio can be swapped, bought or sold on the futures market, and otherwise used to provide offsetting risks for almost any specific investment.

The income function served by the portfolio may be especially critical to smaller banks, since profits in investment activities are often a prime source of profitability. This is true of many large banks, as well, especially since their portfolio volumes are quite large. With tremendous amounts of money to invest, portfolio managers at large banks can make significant contributions to their organizations' earnings.

Investment earnings represent only one reason why a portfolio can be a major contributor to a bank's position. Another factor is that portfolio management is a low-overhead operation. It involves relatively few people, usually just the manager and a few support personnel. Most of the business of managing the portfolio can be handled by telephone or through direct computer connections to the appropriate brokers, traders, investors, and exchanges. There are no advertising or promotion expenses, and fees are generally paid only on transactions that actually transpire. The advantage of generally low overhead is especially noticeable when compared with the high volume of business passing through the portfolio and the profit potential that business represents if properly managed.

For larger banks, the funding facility provided by an investment portfolio is frequently as important as the portfolio's profit potential. The ability to use various instruments in the portfolio to fund extremely large loans, money purchases, and other investment opportunities provides these banks with the flexibility to venture into areas that might otherwise be closed to them. Many portfolio manipulations have little or no adverse effect on the bank's capital position (swaps and futures, for example), which enables the bank to make investment moves that might otherwise be limited by regulatory constraints. The ability to offset most, if not all, of the risk involved in making extremely large loans, for instance, helps the bank provide the full services its customers need, without placing itself in unusually high-risk positions.

An investment portfolio is also important to a bank because it can be manipulated without directly affecting customers at any level. Most other banking activities are personal in that they directly affect customers. If the bank decides that it must increase its return on demand deposit accounts, for example, the only ways to accomplish this are to decrease the services provided on those accounts or increase the fees charged for the services. Either way, bank customers are directly affected, and there is likely to be at least some measure of adverse reaction. The same is true of such actions as increasing loan rates, decreasing rates paid on savings accounts or CDs, and any number of other activities the bank may undertake to increase its earnings or strengthen its position.

Portfolio management, on the other hand, can be done without affecting customer relationships. Swaps, transactions in the futures market, buying or borrowing money, and extending or shortening the maturities of various assets and liabilities are all accomplished by bank personnel. Since most such transactions have virtually no effect on people outside the bank, there is no need to make public whatever portfolio manipulations are required. As long as the bank remains within regulatory restrictions, stays within its stated management objectives, and maintains good relationships with the other parties involved in these manipulations by performing as anticipated, customers and the public in general need not be consulted.

Portfolio Objectives

As noted, the bank's management team must establish specific objectives for its portfolio. These objectives must correspond to what the portfolio *can* do, which includes increasing income through astute investments and providing offsetting instruments to reduce risk, while simultaneously bringing greater potential flexibility to the bank's overall investment strategies. It is critical that objective statements be established and that everyone be made fully aware of them, especially the ALCO, the portfolio manager, and other bank officers and employees who have various investment responsibilities.

If the bank's primary objective is to realize earnings on its investment portfolio, the manager may be given the authority to take greater risks than might otherwise be the case. Such a directive would indicate that the portfolio manager who uses swaps extensively should be more concerned with exchanges that offer greater profit potential than those which are better suited to protecting the bank's liquidity position by extending contractual maturities of liabilities. Similarly, with profit as the primary motive, the manager would look for futures contracts which, if interest rates move as the bank anticipates, do more than offset exposure.

An overall management objective of increasing earnings to the extent possible through manipulation of the investment portfolio requires that the portfolio manager have relatively free reign in his or her activities. The manager must have the *authority*, as well as the responsibility, to take whatever steps appear necessary. Management must realize that the person in charge of the portfolio and its manipulation must have the authority to move quickly and decisively on the bank's behalf.

The portfolio manager and his or her staff also must be fully aware that they are a profit center for the bank. It is likely that their success will rest on their abilities to make money for the bank through astute investments. This stance can result in a great deal of pressure on the individuals involved in portfolio management. Personnel selection becomes critical when earnings are viewed as the most important purpose of portfolio management.

When the primary objective is to assure liquidity at all times, the portfolio manager would probably be more interested in obtaining relatively short-term investments that could, if necessary, be sold on short notice to provide cash. These quick sales can sometimes result in a loss on the investment itself, but they do make it possible to obtain ready cash. If this is the bank's major objective for its portfolio, the manager must act and react accordingly.

With funding as the primary objective, the portfolio manager faces another whole set of possibilities. Under these circumstances, the Financial Planning, Commercial, and other investing departments may well be instructed to go after almost any type of business that meets established credit and other criteria; any risks involved can and are expected

ASSET/LIABILITY MANAGEMENT TECHNIQUES

to be offset by corresponding adjustments in the portfolio. Swaps and futures can then be used extensively to protect the bank against the various exposures resulting from this aggressive investment philosophy. The point is, the investment portfolio can be used to accomplish many different objectives, some of them simultaneously. It is often possible to provide offsetting funding, for example, while still making substantial earnings on the transactions this activity requires. What the portfolio manager needs is a direction, and this is provided by clearly stated objectives from senior management.

To summarize, the bank's management team should take the following steps to assure effective management of its portfolio:

1. *Establish A/L management goals that are acceptable within the framework of the bank's investment philosophy.* These goals must be realistic and attainable in the economic climate within which the bank operates. For instance, in an area in which little if any real estate activity is occurring, it would be unrealistic for the bank to establish an A/L management objective that calls for doubling its mortgage holdings within the next year. But it might be totally realistic to establish an objective that involves hedging every fixed-rate commercial loan that exceeds a specific dollar amount with an offsetting swap or futures contract that protects the bank against exposure. The specific objectives must be based on the bank's current position, where it wants to be in the foreseeable future, and what can be done with its investment portfolio to help reach that goal in an effective, yet efficient, manner.

2. *Communicate those objectives to the appropriate A/L management personnel, most especially the portfolio manager.* These bank

employees and officers will only be able to attain the stated objectives when they know what they are and what activities they are expected to engage in to attain the stated goals. And if those employees' performances are to be judged on the profits they generate for the bank through portfolio activities, they must be made aware of this fact so they can act accordingly.

3. *Determine the strategic role the portfolio is expected to play in attaining the stated objectives.* As previous discussions in this book illustrate, the characteristics of various types of investments can be established fairly accurately. These instruments and tools have well-defined risk characteristics, and market risks will be indicated by the projection mechanisms adopted as part of the overall A/L management strategy. The credit risks presented by many of the investment instruments that are available to the portfolio manager are easier to define than those presented by loans. Further, the instruments at the portfolio manager's disposal are marketable, have maturities that are "adjustable" in the sense that they can be extended or shortened, and provide cash flows that are generally predictable. With all this information available, management should certainly be able to define for the portfolio manager which types of instruments and investment moves he or she is expected to take to accomplish the established objectives.

4. *Define specific needs within the bank that can be satisfied only (or most efficiently) through the investment portfolio.* This helps narrow down the range of activities for the portfolio manager, making the objectives even more meaningful by focusing them on specific needs which management expects the portfolio to satisfy.

ASSET/LIABILITY MANAGEMENT TECHNIQUES

When a portfolio manager receives the proper direction, the manager is able to manipulate the portfolio within the stated policies.

The Necessary Training

Banking has become increasingly dynamic in recent years, especially in regard to investment activities involving asset/liability portfolios. The effects of deregulation have been widespread, resulting in banks' investing in instruments they would have avoided just a few years ago. In addition, whole segments of the industry are constantly on the lookout for new possibilities. New investment instruments are being devised and submitted for regulatory approval on a regular basis. It has become very difficult for a portfolio manager to keep up with all this activity, especially when the workday is frequently hectic and fast-paced.

Every bank must recognize the importance of ongoing training for portfolio managers and their staff. Since this aspect of the industry is moving at such a rapid pace, it is unlikely that internal training will prove sufficient for most banks. The portfolio manager and key staff members probably already know more than most of the bank's officers and employees about investments, types of instruments, and the effects each might have on the bank's position. Therefore, outside training sources must be tapped for the primary players in portfolio management.

Such training is available from a number of sources, including:

- *Large investment houses* whose interests are well served by having bank portfolio managers who are as knowledgeable as possible.

- *Consulting firms* whose primary functions are to provide training seminars and materials on banking matters, including portfolio management.
- *Colleges and universities* with business and/or banking departments that conduct seminars and special classes for professionals.
- *Industry organizations,* including the Bank Administration Institute.
- *Books and magazines* that present the latest theories on portfolio management and the instruments and activities involved.

When the portfolio manager and key staff are kept fully informed as to the objectives of their activities and are trained properly to take the appropriate steps, the bank's objectives are much more likely to be met.

Liquidity and the Portfolio

Methods of establishing the bank's liquidity requirements and sources generally involve establishing a balance between funds sources and uses. This balance is intended to help the bank meet cash requirements as they arise while still enabling it to keep enough money invested at acceptable risks to realize the desired earnings.

Clearly defined liquidity requirements help direct the portfolio manager's investment efforts. The manager must keep liquidity in mind when performing the investment activities required to protect against unacceptable risks while maintaining an acceptable earnings level. When the bank faces known or anticipated liquidity needs, one of the portfolio manager's primary functions is to see that the funds are available.

ASSET/LIABILITY MANAGEMENT TECHNIQUES

An aggressive approach toward satisfying liquidity needs (and, therefore, an equally aggressive approach toward portfolio management) has been taken by many banks today. They have come to look upon the investment portfolio as a source of liquidity *only when no other reasonably priced alternatives are available*. In some respects, this brings an added burden to bear on the portfolio manager, who must make certain that funds can be made available on short notice while recognizing that they may or may not be required of the portfolio.

The liquidity challenge is made even tougher by recent and apparently ongoing swings in customer deposits. Savings account rollovers into CDs, money market, and other investment opportunities, many of them outside the bank, have effectively reduced liquidity sources and have forced many portfolio managers to take alternative action. If the portfolio is thought of as just one part of an integrated A/L management system, some of the pressure is relieved, since the bank can take steps outside the portfolio to offset deposit losses.

Bank management can regard the portfolio/liquidity relationship at either of two levels:

- *Level 1*—the portfolio must be positioned so that it can be used to offset (cover) deposit swings; or,
- *Level 2*—the portfolio is to be used only to satisfy emergency liquidity requirements, rather than as a primary source of liquidity.

With Level 1, the portfolio manager must be constantly aware of the possible need to provide instant liquidity. He or she must therefore limit at least some of the investment activities to very short-term, readily salable instruments. The manager may, in fact, be directed to hold enough such instruments to satisfy liquidity requirements if all or a significant portion of customer deposits are lost to investment competition outside the bank. If so, the manager must be kept informed daily as to the total of these deposits.

Conversely, the bank might assume that customer deposits will remain relatively unchanged or might even increase. It might also be taking an aggressive stance toward bringing more customer money into the bank through a wide range of activities. These activities might include:

- CD sales.
- Money market account sales.
- Increased fee generation for existing services (preferably through increased volume rather than higher fees, although either may apply, especially if competitors' rates have increased).
- Increased fee generation through newly offered services.

Each bank must determine for itself how much it wants to depend on its investment portfolio as a constant source of liquidity. This relates once again to the overall objectives the bank wants to attain with its portfolio. To maximize earnings potential on its investments, the bank should not rely heavily on the portfolio and the instruments it contains to provide most of its required liquidity. Both earnings and the ability to provide certain types of hedges can be curtailed when too much of the portfolio is kept in readily marketable securities for liquidity purposes.

Generally, today's marketplace calls for a reasonably aggressive approach to investment activities. This means that the portfolio manager must be free to take advantage of investments that provide high earnings potential at relatively low risks. Therefore, many banks have adopted a Level 2 approach to liquidity expectations from their investment

ASSET/LIABILITY MANAGEMENT TECHNIQUES

portfolios, relying on them for this purpose only in emergency situations.

With either philosophy concerning how the portfolio should be used to satisfy the bank's liquidity requirements, cash can usually be obtained by selling assets from the portfolio. When asset sales must be made on a "rush" basis to satisfy an emergency liquidity need, excessive losses are sometimes incurred. These losses can be minimized when the portfolio manager is informed in advance that the portfolio might be expected to provide funds to satisfy projected needs at various points. The manager can then plan ahead and have instruments or contingency plans available to meet those needs.

The plans need not involve selling assets or disturbing liabilities in the portfolio. The manager might decide that borrowing Fed funds on an overnight basis makes more sense than taking even a small loss on instruments in the portfolio. Further, contingency plans with cooperator banks can sometimes provide the needed funds with just a phone call. Cooperation in a case such as this can work both ways, and preplanned funds availability agreements between banks can benefit both parties when needs arise.

Finally, several of the management techniques and tools mentioned in this book can provide funds to satisfy liquidity requirements as necessary. For example, buying on the margin in the futures market helps preserve cash, which can then be used to satisfy more immediate liquidity needs should they arise, or for investment purposes if no immediate needs exist. Swaps, too, can sometimes be used to generate funds while still maintaining the overall balance of the portfolio. When the portfolio is regarded as just one element (clearly an important one) of the overall A/L management approach, adequate liquidity sources should be available without having to make constant incursions into the bank's investment package. If an emergency arises, the portfolio manager should be prepared to provide funds without adverse effect on those investments.

Additional Portfolio Management Concepts

Beyond the information already covered, the portfolio manager should be aware of several other concepts that might help to do a more effective job. Some of these are expansions of thoughts previously presented, while others have not yet been discussed. The objective here is to provoke additional thinking as to steps that might work in managing a bank's investment portfolio.

- *To the extent possible, expand the bank's investment "menu."* The new types of securities mentioned earlier just might fit into the organization's investment philosophy and work to the bank's advantage. A greater selection of investment opportunities enables the portfolio manager to find instruments that provide higher yields without significantly increasing risks. Money market securities, corporate securities, and various types of floating-rate investments are available today that were simply not considered in bank portfolio planning just a few years ago. Some of these might fit into the bank's plans better at one time than another, so the fact that a proposed investment is rejected as an alternative at one time does not necessarily mean that it would not work perfectly well under different circumstances. This ties in with the manager's keeping abreast of what is happening in the industry. By knowing what new investment opportunities are available, the manager can make a realistic recommendation when it seems that one or more of them might satisfy a particular requirement.

- *The portfolio manager (and staff, if applicable) must be totally aware of and capable of analyzing credit risks.* Many times, the person in charge of the portfolio has extensive experience and expertise in investment activities, but has had little or no training in judging credit risks. As noted earlier, training in such areas as credit evaluation may be necessary as efforts are made to expand the portfolio's investment opportunities into additional areas.

- *The portfolio manager must be aware of funding costs for various types of investments.* This means that the manager must be apprised of where the funds for investing come from. This helps the manager identify the costs of the funds which, in turn, makes it possible to make more intelligent investments. If an offsetting swap or futures contract appears to be advisable for a certain instrument, the more the portfolio manager knows about that instrument, including the potential yield it represents, the more efficiently and effectively he or she can function.

- *The portfolio manager can enhance the value of the portfolio by not over-diversifying.* While this discussion has suggested broadening the portfolio base by taking advantage of more investment opportunities, including new instruments as they are developed and become available, too many small items make the portfolio difficult to manage. Having too many instruments can also make it more difficult to attain and/or maintain a specific asset or liability position. While diversification is a good way to maintain earnings and minimize risks, it is often accomplished more effectively with a few larger instruments and transactions than with a greater number of smaller instruments of various types. Larger blocks are generally easier to sell or trade should this become necessary or advantageous.

- *The manager must be aware of the yields provided by various instruments and fund types.* These yields vary with prevailing interest rates, so there is no way to establish a specific dollar yield that will always be provided by a given investment. The portfolio manager must be aware of the yield that can be realized on various instruments at prevailing rates. It is not enough to know the cost of funds; their yields are just as important to a portfolio manager in the effort to protect and enhance the bank's position.

- *The bank's overall income picture can be improved by using the portfolio to obtain additional funding.* Repurchase agreements with investment houses and brokers allow the bank to obtain funding that might otherwise be unavailable. The government agency element of the portfolio can be used to lend to dealer institutions. While the return on such funds is usually not spectacular (often around 50 basis points between REPOs and Fed funds), those funds might otherwise lie idle or might even be ignored by the bank. REPOs can also be used to free refund securities, enabling the bank to take advantage of market cycles. The bank can buy at opportune times, then sell when rates have reached the appropriate point, thereby increasing earnings.

Several other specific steps can be taken both to improve earnings and to assure liquidity. For example, bond lending can be used. One bank "lends" a bond to another bank that has a specific, often pressing need for that security. A fee of 40 to 50 basis points per day is charged by the "lending" bank until the other institution is in a position to return the bond to the original bank. In addition, the lender receives another security from the second bank—a security that is of similar quality and greater market value than the one being "loaned."

In these respects, bond lending is similar to a secured loan transaction; a fee is charged for the service (corresponding to loan interest), and the security received in exchange serves as collateral. But an additional advantage is provided with this type of transaction. Since a security exchange takes place, this is an off-balance sheet transaction that does not restrict either bank's capital. These transactions are consistent income producers for the portfolio, due to the basis point advantage provided. And the "borrowing" bank, by exchanging one security for another, has not actually borrowed funds. Its capital position also is unaffected, since an immediate "swap" of securities has occurred.

Activities such as these are handled either through a dealer or directly with a correspondent bank. While bond and other securities "lending" of this type can produce a consistent, surprisingly high income for the portfolio, they can be dangerous from a credit standpoint. The portfolio manager must be alert to (and trained to evaluate) the credit of the correspondent bank and other parties involved (dealers, if applicable). If the manager does not have this expertise, he or she should have ready access to the experts at the bank who can help make such credit decisions relatively quickly.

The Portfolio and the Tax Position

One final consideration to be made in portfolio management is the bank's tax position. The portfolio manager must be constantly aware of the prevailing tax regulations. Since this is just one aspect of the job, the manager must have the advice of bank personnel who remain knowledgeable concerning these tax regulations. Otherwise, an investment the portfolio manager assumes will add to earnings through tax advantages may turn out to cost more than other investments that are clearly taxable.

In general, the most recent tax laws have eliminated many of the tax-free investments that were once available to banks. The government has offset some of the losses resulting from these regulations by lowering the maximum corporate tax rate. Through all these changes, it is easy for a portfolio manager to miscalculate the tax-free nature of specific types of securities. For this reason, through the ALCO and the various departments of the bank, the portfolio manager must be kept informed as to which investments provide tax situations that enhance the bank's overall position.

Summary

The key to successful portfolio management is making sure that the manager knows exactly what is expected of him or her and of the portfolio itself. The bank that is interested primarily in generating income from its investment portfolio will provide totally different directions than one that is most interested in investment safety. While no bank wants to take undue risks in its investment activities, one that anticipates the highest possible earnings from its portfolio will expect the manager to look for higher-yield investments, and these almost always entail somewhat greater risks than securities providing low yields. Conversely, the bank that is most interested in making low-risk investments, even if this means some measure of sacrifice in potential earnings, will provide different directions to its portfolio manager.

There is merit to each of these philosophies. One bank's management may have made it clear that it prefers low risk to potentially greater earnings, while the opposite might be

ASSET/LIABILITY MANAGEMENT TECHNIQUES

the case in another bank. Either way, the portfolio manager must be apprised of management's desires and then must manipulate the investments in the portfolio accordingly.

The same concepts apply to the bank's liquidity expectations of its portfolio. If the bank expects a high percentage of its liquidity needs to be satisfied by the portfolio, the manager must concentrate on types of instruments that can be sold readily, preferably on a planned basis to avoid loss. This restricts the manager's investment activities, in a sense, because they must devote more of the portfolio to items that can be used as liquidity sources. But this is not necessarily "bad," since the portfolio can be used very effectively to satisfy ongoing liquidity needs.

The other approach is to provide the bulk of the bank's liquidity through other sources—fees generated, consumer loans, deposits, CDs, and the like. The portfolio can then be used only as necessary to provide emergency liquidity should the bank face a need that cannot be satisfied through those other sources. Here, the portfolio manager has greater flexibility in investment activities, since the objective is to seek investments that provide higher yields, but which are not necessarily quickly convertible to cash. These decisions all hinge on the bank's policy toward the portfolio and its uses. Once that policy is clearly stated, it is up to the portfolio manager to conduct investment activities accordingly.

Senior management must keep the ALCO, the portfolio manager, and all other personnel who are involved in investment activities informed as to the prevailing bank policies. These personnel can only do an effective job when they know what their objectives are. How they meet those objectives is often up to them, as long as they remain within the overall guidelines of bank policy and the applicable banking regulations.

Swaps, futures, and perhaps even options can play an important role in portfolio management. The bank can buy and sell on the margin, then plan ahead to meet whatever obligations exist as they arise. It also can anticipate when to buy and sell various instruments based on the established objectives.

Regardless of the role senior management expects the investment portfolio to play, these key points are always applicable:

- The portfolio managers and their staff must be kept informed as to their objectives.

- They must have access to the expertise that exists in-house in every bank—credit, lending, planning, and financial experts who can advise the manager concerning actions that can and should be taken.

- Portfolio management must be thought of as just one segment, albeit an important one, of the overall A/L management effort.

With these critical steps accomplished, portfolio management can be handled effectively in any banking situation or economic environment.

Conclusion

Asset and liability management represents one of the most important means by which a bank can establish and maintain a favorable earnings position. Through adept manipulation of its investment portfolio, it can control the gap between rate-sensitive assets and rate-sensitive liabilities, thereby assuring that its position is protected no matter how volatile market interest rates become.

It would be impractical to protect any institution against every imaginable risk. To do so would require such a conservative attitude that virtually no risks could be tolerated; consequently, very little (if any) return would be realized on the bank's investments. The optimum situation is to manage the investment portfolio in such a way that acceptable risks are tolerated in exchange for a reasonable return on funds invested. The tools, techniques, and concepts presented in this book are intended to help the bank, its ALCO, the portfolio manager, and the rest of its investment and marketing staff do just that.

To obtain the greatest return on investments while keeping risks within acceptable limits, senior management must establish specific objectives it wishes to attain with the bank's portfolio. These objectives must then be communicated to the personnel who must obtain the desired results. Investment staff members, including the portfolio manager, must be given sufficient flexibility to apply their expertise toward meeting the stated goals. These steps enable the portfolio manager to function effectively within the framework of the bank's stated investment policy.

One approach is to require that, for every major asset and liability (or block of them) acquired, a matching instru-

ASSET/LIABILITY MANAGEMENT TECHNIQUES

ment be introduced into the portfolio. The matching techniques discussed in this book enable the bank to maintain approximately the same A/L gap at all times. This approach limits portfolio managers to some extent, since they must be more concerned with hedging the bank's exposure to loss with matching instruments than with taking advantage of potentially higher-yield investment opportunities. On the other hand, a matching policy frees the New Business, Lending, Planning, and other departments within the bank to move ahead with whatever types of business they wish (within the framework of the bank's overall policies), since virtually any loan that is made or any security that is obtained is matched with offsetting instruments in the portfolio. This "safest" approach may restrict the bank to a lower overall return on its investments, but it also protects it against potentially severe losses.

With or without a matching policy as a guideline, a portfolio manager may be able to use swaps, futures, and options to protect against potential risks. These instruments can also be used to obtain greater yields when the manager is not confined to a strict matching philosophy. In either event, these tools are well within the reach (financially) of most small banks. They provide the portfolio manager with investment opportunities that can provide positive rewards.

Liquidity concerns represent another dimension for the portfolio manager. If management expects the portfolio to provide a constant source of funds to satisfy liquidity needs, the manager must maintain more readily negotiable instruments in the portfolio than otherwise. These instruments often provide a lower yield than longer-term investments that are less readily marketable. Still, a portfolio that consists primarily (or in significant part) of assets and liabilities that can be marketed quickly at minimal losses can be

CONCLUSION

profitable, with proper planning and sufficient advance notice of liquidity requirements.

A more aggressive approach is to expect the portfolio to serve as a source of quick liquidity only in emergency situations. The bank looks to other sources, such as customer deposits, CDs, and money market accounts, to satisfy day-to-day liquidity needs. With this less demanding approach, the portfolio manager can maintain enough instruments that can be marketed quickly at no or minimal losses to help the bank through short-term liquidity crises. With this "emergency-only" directive toward liquidity, the manager can place greater emphasis on portfolio profitability, thereby making a more significant contribution to overall earnings.

The swap technique can enhance earnings and provide interest rate risk protection by allowing the manager to locate and trade for instruments that offset those obtained by the bank, often at a profit. Correspondents in swap transactions can include other banks and investment houses. When other banks are involved, they are frequently looking for offsetting instruments that satisfy their own portfolio needs. A swap can usually be effected for almost any instrument or block of instruments a bank wants to trade, frequently through a regional money center bank. When an investment house handles a swap transaction, speculators may be involved—investors who feel that the instruments in question will make them money. Either way, swaps represent an effective means of protecting against potential losses while realizing earnings on various investment instruments.

Futures and options can broaden the portfolio manager's investment horizons even further. By buying and selling on the margin in the futures market, the manager can protect the bank's cash position, retaining liquidity and invest-

ASSET/LIABILITY MANAGEMENT TECHNIQUES

ment capital while hedging risks and increasing profit potential. With both futures and options, the exact steps to be taken are dictated by the market and the bank's relative position at the time.

Successful portfolio management is most easily accomplished when it is viewed as just one part of an overall A/L management effort. The bank's entire investment, lending, and general business philosophy must be considered when establishing the guidelines under which the portfolio manager is to function. Most important are these key points:

- The portfolio manager and his or her staff must be fully apprised of the bank's expectations from its investments.
- Constant training and retraining of the portfolio manager and staff must be undertaken to help them stay abreast of trends in the industry, new instruments as they become available, and so on.
- Daily follow-up and direction from management and the ALCO should be an integral part of A/L and portfolio management.
- As needs change, the portfolio manager must be kept aware of shifts in investment philosophy and the bank's preferred approach to investment management. This enables the manager to do an effective job of making the portfolio keep pace with the bank's requirements.

There are no secret formulas to successful asset/liability or portfolio management. The manager's position requires constant vigilance and might be considered by many to be a pressure-packed assignment. In many ways, it is; but the rewards of effective portfolio and overall A/L management, both personally and to the bank, make this environment well worthwhile to those who engage in it regularly.

CONCLUSION

It is hoped that the information in this book provides a solid base from which the A/L manager can work. Not every idea has been touched upon, nor can that special touch known as *creativity* be provided on the pages of a book. For the right person, A/L management represents an outstanding opportunity to grow with a bank. The information presented on these pages will help attain that goal.

Index

A

Accounting considerations
options, 107
swaps, 48–50
Asset and liability
committee (ALCO), 2, 111
Assets, matching with
liabilities
definition, 7–9
generally, 3, 131, 132
"matching" defined, 7, 8
techniques, 7–25; Fig. 1;
Table 1

B

Basis and basis risk,
66–69; Fig. 6
Basis rate swaps, 28, 29.
See also Swaps

C

Call options. *See* Options
Cash flow calculations, use
in swaps, 39
Conversion factor hedge
technique, 83–87; Figs.
9, 10
Credit considerations in
swaps, 42–45

Credit risk analysis, need
for, 124
Cross-currency agreements
in swaps, 50
Currency coupon swaps,
28, 29. *See also* Swaps
Custom options, 99, 100.
See also Options

D

Deferred takedown or
rate-setting in swaps, 50
Duration analysis
technique (of gap
measurement), 9, 16, 17
Duration hedge technique,
88–91; Fig. 11

E

Early termination
penalties, 39
Earnings, projections, 1–3
Exchange-traded and
custom options, 99, 100.
See also Options

F

Fixed-rate currency swaps,
28, 29. *See also* Swaps

Formula approach (to measuring interest rate risk), 47, 48; Table 4
Forward agreements, 53–57
Futures
   as forward agreements, 55, 56
   comparison to swaps, 64–66
   definition, 53, 54
   generally, 3, 4, 133, 134
   hedge ratios, 76–82; Figs. 7, 8
   implementation, 57–60; Fig. 5
   interest rates on 60, 61
   techniques, 53–93; Figs. 5–11

G

Gap, asset/liability
   generally, 2
   measurement and projection techniques, 9–20; Fig. 1; Table 1
Gap profile approach (to gap measurement), 9, 12–15; Fig. 1; Table 1

H

Hedge ratios
   for futures, 71, 76–82; Figs. 7, 8
   for options, 105
Hedges
   conversion factor, 83–87; Figs. 9, 10
   duration, 88–92; Fig. 11
   using options as, 103–107

I

Interest rate swaps. *See* Swaps
Interest rates on futures contracts, 60
Investment "menu" expansion, 123
Investment portfolios
   diversification, 124
   liquidity of, 119–123
   objectives of, 114–118
   roles of, 112–114
   tax considerations, 126, 127
   training in managing, 118, 119
   use to obtain additional funding, 125

L

Liabilities, matching with assets. *See* Assets, matching with liabilities

Liquidity considerations
in futures contracts, 62, 63, 71
in matching techniques, 9, 22, 23
in the portfolio, 119–123, 132, 133

M

Maintenance margins, 59

Mark-to-market method, 49, 50

Matching assets and liabilities. *See* Assets, matching with liabilities

Money market instruments, use in futures, 73

N

National swap code, 39–42

"Notional principal" concept, 27, 29

O

Options
accounting for, 107
definition, 95
determining status of, 100–102
generally, 4, 95–103, 133, 134; Fig. 12
use as hedges, 103–107

P

Picou, Dr. Glenn, 79, 84

Portfolios. *See* Investment portfolios

Profiles, gap. *See* Gap profile approach

Projection approach (to measuring interest rate risk), 46, 47

Put options. *See* Options

R

Risk
basis, 66–69; Fig. 6
credit, 124
in futures contracts, 71, 72
interest rate, 1–3, 46–48; Table 4

S

Settlement accounting, 48, 49

Simulation technique (of gap measurement), 9, 16

Swaps
    advantages of, 32–35; Fig. 3
    comparison to futures, 64–66
    generally, 3, 27, 29–31, 133; Fig. 2
    implementation, 39–42
    structures, 28, 29
    techniques, 27–52; Figs. 2–4; Tables 2–4

T

Takedown, deferred, 50
Tax considerations of portfolio, 126, 127

U

Unrealized loss accounting, 49, 50

V

Variable rates in swaps, 50
Variation margins, 59